People I Want to
Punch in the Throat

People I Want to Punch in the Throat

Competitive Crafters, Drop-Off Despots, and Other Suburban Scourges

Jen Mann

BALLANTINE BOOKS TRADE PAPERBACKS

NEW YORK

A Ballantine Books Trade Paperback Original

Copyright © 2014 by Jen Mann

Published in the United States by Ballantine Books, an imprint of
Random House, a division of Random House LLC, a Penguin Random
House Company, New York.

BALLANTINE and the HOUSE colophon are registered trademarks of
Random House LLC.

LIBRARY OF CONGRESS CATALOGING-IN-PUBLICATION DATA

Mann, Jen.
People I want to punch in the throat : competitive crafters, drop-off
despots, and other suburban scourges / Jen Mann.
pages   cm
ISBN 978-0-345-54983-9 (paperback)—ISBN 978-0-345-54998-3 (ebook)
1. Suburban life—Humor.   2. Suburbanites—United States—Humor.
I. Title.
PN6231.S8M36 2014
818'.602—dc23   2014024031

Printed in the United States of America on acid-free paper

www.ballantinebooks.com

9 8 7 6 5 4 3 2 1

Book design by Caroline Cunningham

This book is dedicated to the Hubs.

You must love me if you were willing to

move to the suburbs.

Contents

Author's Note ix

People I Want to Punch in the Throat: A Short List 3

You've Got Mail! 5

Take Your Mother's Sandwich and Shove It 23

The Hubs or the Cleaning Lady—Don't Make Me Choose 32

God Bless America (and Thongs) 44

Just Some of the Many Reasons the Neighbors
    Always Hate Us 52

Screw Your Playgroup, I Didn't Want to Join Anyway 58

Gomer Might Be a Racist 65

Jeez, Lady, I Just Wanted a Cup of Coffee, Not Your
    Kidney 73

Hello Mother, Hello Father, Signing Up for Camp Sucks 79

Ooh, Sorry to Hear You Got Agnes in Your Class,
 but I Hear Her Mother Is Lovely 88

Thou Shalt Not Covet Thy Neighbor's Sweet-Ass Ride 103

Am I Supposed to Believe a Five-Year-Old Made That? 108

Carpool Lines and Bunny Pajamas Go Together Like . . .
 Nothing. They Don't Go Together at All. 119

The Husband Inquisition 127

Who Needs Dr. Phil When We Have Adolpha? 132

Do You Ever Invite Me Over When You're Not Trying
 to Sell Me Something? 142

Sleepover Is Not a Party Theme! And Other Stupid
 Things Suburban Moms Complain About 149

It's Free Bowling, Lady, Not the Junior Olympics 158

I Thought Mother's Little Helper Was a Babysitter.
 I Was Wrong—It's Drugs. 163

Motherhood: The Toughest Competition You'll
 Ever Judge 170

Watch It, That Room Mom'll Cut You 183

Would You Take Less than a Quarter for
 This Swarovski Vase? 190

Moms' Night Out at the Gun Range 201

Acknowledgments 207

Author's Note

All of the names and identifying characteristics of the people who appear in this book have been changed to protect the good, the bad, and the ugly. So if you think you see yourself in the pages, please be assured that you are almost certainly wrong. These are my stories and this is how I remember them.

People I Want to
Punch in the Throat

PEOPLE I WANT TO PUNCH IN THE THROAT: A SHORT LIST

My parents. Seriously, who spells their kid's name "Jenni" with an adorable *i*? I guess they never expected me to be a doctor.

Anyone who thinks I really named my kids Gomer and Adolpha. Their real names are actually worse.

That one guy who sits in the middle of Starbucks yelling into his stupid Bluetooth about a bullshit quarterly report. We all hope you choke on your latte.

Extreme couponers who hold up the checkout line over thirty frickin' cents. I'm mostly pissed off because I always forget my coupons at home.

People who treat their pets like children. No further explanation needed.

Anyone who feels the need to bling her washer and dryer. I blame Pinterest for this shit.

The guy in front of me at McDonald's the other day who asked, "What's good here?" Even the guy behind the counter didn't know how to answer.

Humblebraggers. If you have something to brag about, then just own it.

Anyone who names their kid after a Kardashian or a *Twilight* character. Trust me, no one believes that you just "thought up" the name North on your own.

Moms who tell me my life would be so much easier if I implemented "systems." Oh, fuck you.

People who tell me not to swear so much. Oh, fuck you, too.

People who think this book might be about them. Don't be so vain. You're not the only asshat I know.

YOU'VE GOT MAIL!

Believe it or not, I'm happily married to a guy who doesn't mind the fact that I've never set foot in a CrossFit class and that I own "good" Crocs and "bad" Crocs. He overlooks my unfortunate shoe choice and I don't mind that he follows me through the house flipping off lights to save money or gets his hair cut only when he has a coupon.

I know right about now you're feeling some twinges of jealousy. You're thinking to yourself: "That sounds like a match made in heaven!" or "How do I catch a guy like that?" Well, let me tell you how we met.

In 1996 or so, I bought my first home computer. It was some sort of IBM product. If I was some weird computer nerd, I would be able to tell you all about the ROM and RAM this machine had. All I know is that it was black when every other model was off-white. When I was perusing models with the sales guy who was blathering on and on about what it could do, all I could think was how much better the black would look in my home office than the ugly off-white. I'm *that* kind of nerd.

I needed a computer because I was going to write a novel, you see. Ha! I'm still stuck on the first sentence: *It was a dark and stormy night. . . .*

I got the computer home and unpacked it and found that it included a disk, or was it a disc? I can't remember. Anyway, it was for a free trial of America Online. Remember AOL? I'm sure the Internet had been around for years at that point, but I'd been at school in Bumblefuck, Iowa, where I barely had phone service, let alone Internet, and as I stated above, I was not a computer nerd (just a regular nerd), so I didn't know what the hell AOL was exactly. I read the description and decided I should try it. For someone like me, who really couldn't comprehend the Internet, it sounded like the perfect introduction.

I hooked up my computer, plugged it into a phone jack, and went online for the first time. These were the days of dial-up, so I'd log in and send AOL off to find an open line, and then I'd have time to get some dinner, put on my jammies, and maybe even throw in a load of laundry before I'd hear: *"You've got mail!"*

AOL was so smart. Even the first time I logged in I had mail. It was just a welcome letter from them, but it was still mail and I loved to hear that voice announce every time I logged on. It was like crack for me. I was hooked. So long, social life!

Ha! As if I really had a social life to lose! In those days, I was living on my own and working at a shitty job. Most of my friends were married at that point and I didn't feel like being a third wheel. My life was pretty much: get up, go to work, come home, watch whatever crappy show was on TV (this was before DVRs, so you had to watch whatever was on plus the commercials—it totally sucked balls), and go to bed. Get up the next day and repeat.

I quickly discovered that many people went on AOL to "chat." There were tons of chat rooms to choose from based on your interests. Everything from dog grooming to knitting to S&M. You could also search through profiles to see who was online and send them an instant message (IM) to see if they wanted to chat privately.

For the first few weeks I would jump around from one chat room to another. Every time you entered a chat room somebody would IM you with "a/s/l?" That's douchebag-speak for age/sex/location. The hard-core douchebags would add "What are you wearing?" to the list. The annoying thing was, all of this information was in my profile (except my attire), but those dipshits were too lazy to look. It just seemed so show-us-your-tits to me. Ugh.

As soon as I'd enter a chat room, I'd get bombarded with IMs asking me my age and location. I was very popular, and I couldn't figure out why, because this had never been the case in the outside world. I'd reply, and then half the time the next question was: "What are you wearing?" I didn't know enough to lie, so I'd reply: "Sweatpants." My chat partner would go silent. Not the answer they were hoping for I guess.

I tried a local chat room a couple of times. Supposedly everyone in that room lives in the same city, and you go there mostly to hook up with local strangers. It creeped me out, because I didn't like the idea of "running into" someone I might actually know. I could just see my neighbor IMing me, "a/s/l/naked?" The guys in the local rooms also put a lot of pressure on you to meet IRL (in real life), so I tended to stay away.

I liked hanging out in the twentysomethings room, which was full of, well, twentysomething people from all over the world. Most of the people in there were cool and they never asked me if I was naked or if I wanted to meet IRL. I spent many evenings chatting/typing with people.

One night I entered the twentysomethings chat room and I received an IM from a guy who asked my name and age. Ugh. *Can't you read?* I thought. But instead I told him, "Jen, 24." I waited for "What are you wearing?" but it didn't come. Instead we had a really normal conversation. Well, as normal as a conversation can be when you're typing to a stranger halfway across the country. He told me his name was Ebenezer. He was a year older than me and lived in Queens, New York, and had just graduated from NYU's film school. We chatted about movies and current events and made each other laugh. A lot. He was really funny and dry. Sometimes humor is hard to convey when you can't hear the tone, but I totally got his sense of humor.

He especially made me laugh when he asked about my screen name.

Ebenezer: Tell me about your name.

Jen: My name? I dunno. My parents gave it to me.

Ebenezer: No. Not your real name. Your screen name. It's . . . interesting.

Jen: It is?

Ebenezer: Yes. I'm curious about it. How did you come up with it?

Jen: Well, I'm a writer, you know.

Ebenezer: Yes. You mentioned that.

Jen: And names are very important to writers. They give them a lot of thought.

Ebenezer: Did you give your screen name a lot of thought?

Jen: Of course! (I didn't want to tell him, but I thought my screen name was extremely witty. I had worked very hard on coming up with an excellent screen name.)

Ebenezer: So, how did you think of it?

Jen: Well, I used my name: Jen. Duh.

Ebenezer: Duh.

Jen: And then I incorporated my [at that time] favorite book: Douglas Coupland's *Generation X*. Remember, I told you I think he's a genius and totally the voice of our generation. He just gets us. Y'know? (On a side note, I just Googled Douglas Coupland to make sure I was spelling his name correctly, and holy hell! He is an old man. Am I that old? Shit. We are so damn old, Generation X!)

Ebenezer: Yes, yes. Maybe one of these days I'll finally read that book.

Jen: OK, so I took Jen and *Generation X* and I wanted my screen name to be JenX. Get it?

Ebenezer: I think so. Is it like Malcolm X?

Jen: Nooo, silly!

Ebenezer: LOL. J/K.

Jen: I'm Jen. I'm Generation X. I'm JenX.

Ebenezer: OK, but that's not your screen name.

Jen: No. Because AOL said JenX was already taken, so they offered me Jenexxx. I was disappointed I was late to the name game, but then I decided AOL's suggestion was perfect.

Go ahead, laugh at me. I know you can see what I did there—even if I couldn't. I've told you numerous times I'm an idiot.

Ebenezer: So instead of JenX, you took Jenexxx. You don't see that those two names are different?

Jen: What do you mean? They're both just variations of the same name.

Ebenezer: They're not. One is VERY different.

Jen: I don't understand.

Ebenezer: Jen X or Jene XXX.

Jen: OH SHIT!

Ebenezer: Ahhh. Now you see it.

Jen: Now I see why you wanted to talk to me!

Ebenezer: At first, yes. Kind of. But then you were funny and I liked talking to you.

Jen: Aren't you going to ask me what I'm wearing?

Ebenezer: I assume sweatpants.

The next day I logged on and I heard "You've got mail!" It was an email from Ebenezer telling me he had enjoyed our talk and he hoped we could chat again soon. I wrote back. I don't remember what I wrote. I probably said something like, "I'm not that stupid usually and I'm not a porn star, either, so if you think we're going to have cybersex, you're crazy." And I'm sure he responded with, "Seriously, don't flatter yourself. No one even mentioned cybersex. What is your damage?" This started an email exchange, and when we'd see each other online we'd chat.

He became my "friend," if you can say that about someone you've never met. I didn't even know what he looked like. His screen name was Ebenezer11423, and for the longest time I imagined he was a nice Jewish boy from NYU. It wasn't until after countless emails back and forth that while we were IMing one day, he casually mentioned he was Chinese.

Jenexxx: Wait. You're Chinese?

Ebenezer11423: Yup. You got a problem with that?

Jenexxx: No. I just didn't know you were Chinese.

Ebenezer11423: I didn't realize it was a big deal. I didn't think it was a big deal that you're white. You are white, right?

Jenexxx: Yes, I'm white. It's not a big deal. I just imagined you were, too.

Ebenezer11423: Why?

Jenexxx: I don't know. I guess I went with the straight-up stereotype: Queens, NYU film school, and a Hebrew name. My mind didn't immediately go to Chinese guy.

Ebenezer11423: Is this going to be a problem?

Jenexxx: Relax. Of course it's not a problem. But just so you know, I am totally not attracted to Chinese guys, so we definitely won't ever have cybersex.

Ebenezer11423: Hey, not to worry. I'm not attracted to girls in sweatpants, so it's all good.

I found myself looking forward to hearing from Ebenezer and chatting with him. We talked a lot about our shitty jobs and our dreams of one day being paid for our creativity.

There was never any pressure to meet because he lived in New York and I lived in Kansas. It was a perfect pen pal situation.

Until December. When I was growing up in New Jersey, my parents would always take me and my brother, C.B., into New York City to see the Christmas lights. We hadn't been back in several years, and that year they decided to make a family trip.

At first I thought, *Ugh, a trip with my parents? I'm twenty-four years old—I should* not *be going on a trip with my parents and my twenty-year-old brother!* But then my parents sweetened the deal. They offered to pay and take me to a Broadway play. I am a total sucker for *Les Misérables*—you really can't see it too many times—so of course I agreed to go.

I debated whether to tell Ebenezer that I was going to visit New York City. I really liked being pen pals and I didn't want to ruin it all by meeting. But then again, how stupid was it to visit his city and not call? It seemed so odd. Were we friends or not?

I decided to tell him I was coming for a long weekend and we should meet for coffee.

He freaked out. His exact words were:

Ebenezer11423: If you think I'm taking you out on a date, you're crazy.

Jenexxx: Whoa. Easy, killer. Who said I wanted to go on a date with you?

Ebenezer11423: I know you. You just go out with guys so you can get a free meal.

Jenexxx: Relax. Nobody said anything about a date. All I said was we've been emailing each other for months, I'm finally going to be in your city, and wouldn't it be nice to meet for coffee so we can put a face with the emails?

Ebenezer11423: I'll think about it and let you know.

Jenexxx: Never mind. Forget I asked. Don't do me any favors.

I was mortified and pissed off all at the same time. Who did this guy think he was? No one had said anything about a date. Everyone knows coffee is not a date. What a fucking asshole! We didn't chat again for a few more days. Finally, I received an email from him laying out the ground rules for our meeting:

Jen,

I have to work on Friday, but I can come to your hotel at 6 pm. Since 6 pm is kind of late for coffee and I'll be hungry, we should meet for dinner. We'll go someplace fun and unique to NYC. A place I'm sure you don't have in Kansas. It's called TGI Fridays.

We can go to dinner—you'll need to bring money and pay for your own meal because this is NOT A DATE and I'm pretty busy that night, so don't think I'm going to take you on a tour of Manhattan or anything like that. I'm NOT a tour guide. If you're cool or whatever we could go get some ice cream or something after, but if you're boring I'll warn you there is a new episode of *Homicide* on that night and I'm not going to miss it if you're boring, so I'll just leave.

If you want to go, let me know. Here's my pager number.

Ebenezer

To this day I am completely amazed I went to dinner with this yahoo. Either there had to be divine intervention or I was desperate to have potato skins without my parents. I still haven't decided which it was. All I know is, I was glad Ebenezer was willing to give up his *Homicide* night, because I wouldn't have given up my tickets to see *Les Mis* and I would never have gone to dinner with him and his life would be so boring now.

I wish I *would have* replied with the following:

Dear Ebenezer,

Where do I begin? TGI Fridays? Are you for real? You're absolutely right. This is NOT a date. Especially if you are taking me to TGI Fridays. Are they so popular in New York City that you are delusional enough to think this is fine dining? Mozzarella sticks and wings are some of the best fare they have to offer. Plus, you do know that's a chain restaurant, right? There is one right down the street from my house. While I do live in Kansas, I don't live in a sod house, so believe it or not, I have been to this classy establishment you mentioned and I'm not impressed. It is neither "fun" nor "unique."

Honestly, I think dinner is a bit too much. That's why I suggested coffee. Because it can be done in 15 minutes. And if I think YOU'RE boring I won't have to sit through an entire meal with you AND spend nine bucks.

And why do you have a pager? Are you a drug dealer?

> Sincerely,
> Jen

Instead I replied with:

E—Don't be such an asshole and don't overthink it. You're right, it's not a date, so just relax and stop being such an idiot. You're embarrassing yourself. Six will work for me and I'm sure I'll have you home in plenty of time for *Homicide.* J

The day of our non-date, I finally told my parents what I was doing. "You're meeting a man from the Internet?" my mom asked.

"Oh God, you are so desperate, aren't you?" C.B. laughed.

"Shut up, C.B. You have to go and get your picture taken on Santa's lap by yourself," I sneered.

"What? Is that true, Mom? We're doing that tonight?"

"Shush, C.B. I told you at breakfast that was on the agenda for tonight. Don't worry about that now. It will be fun. Let's talk about Jenni and this boyfriend of hers."

"He's not my boyfriend. We're just friends online."

"Does he know what you look like?" my dad asked.

"Kind of. I sent him a picture once. But it was kind of old. It was from college."

"Have you seen a picture of him?" my mom asked.

"Well . . ." Shit. I hadn't. I started to think of all the reasons he'd given me for not sending a picture: his camera was broken, he didn't have a scanner, he never takes pictures, he didn't have a stamp to mail me a picture from college . . . I was getting catfished, before catfishing was a thing. "No. But it doesn't matter what he looks like. It's. Not. A. Date."

"Well, how will you recognize him?" Mom asked.

"He's meeting me here in the hotel lobby. He's going to wear a dark green Kenneth Cole jacket so I'll be able to recognize him."

"Okay," my dad said, "let's just break this down. You're going to dinner—dutch—at TGI Fridays with a Chinese guy from Queens named Ebenezer who has a pager and will be wearing a dark green Kenneth Cole jacket and will meet you in the lobby at six o'clock tonight?"

"Yes, that sounds right."

"And you swear you're not desperate?" C.B. cackled.

"Go put on your nice Christmas sweater, C.B. The one that matches Mommy's! You're going to look adorable on Santa's lap. I hope they buy the picture so Mom can put it in with her Christmas letter this year."

"Well, if you're not desperate, Jenni, then can you tell us why you're meeting this stranger?" my mom inquired.

"I don't know. He's just someone I like to talk to. He listens to me and he laughs at me and he makes me laugh. He's fun. I just thought it would be cool to finally meet and put a face with the words. Maybe it's desperate, but it's better than waiting on line at Macy's for three hours to see a perv in a Santa suit!"

"Okay, okay. We're just a little worried. Girls end up dead from meeting men online. I saw it on *Dateline*," Mom said.

"I'm pretty sure he's not going to kill me. If anything, I think he's going to stand me up."

"Why would you think that?" my dad wondered.

"I dunno. 'Cause he's kind of a jerk."

"Wow. He sounds like a keeper!" crowed C.B.

"Hey! Let me know how the romantic horse-drawn carriage ride through Central Park goes, C.B. You know Mom and Dad will snuggle you in between them, right?"

"We're doing *that* tonight, too?"

"I bet you wish you had a 'keeper' to meet now, don't you, C.B.?"

"You're a grown woman. We can't stop you, but at least leave us his pager number and whatever description you have of him," my dad said.

Dad got the safety issues out of the way so that Mom could focus on the important task at hand: "What are you wearing tonight?"

Yeah, so this is the part of the story that gets a bit embarrassing (as if it hasn't already been embarrassing). I wore overalls to our non-date. There were several factors that went into picking out my ensemble for that night. It was partly a "fuck you" to Ebenezer for being such an asshole and making me feel like shit by emphasizing a bajillion times that we weren't going on a date. As far as I was concerned, he didn't deserve a nicer outfit. It was partly an ironic thing. I thought it was funny that the girl from Kansas would wear overalls. It was exactly what a snooty New Yorker would expect a Kansan to wear. It was subtle and deep all at the same time. And it was partly a comfort thing. I do enjoy

TGI Fridays's potato skins, and overalls are the perfect pants when you've got a potato-skin food baby to hide.

I should have known that night as soon as I saw Ebenezer in my hotel lobby that I was in trouble. *Damn,* I thought. *He's really cute. Who would have thought? Shit, maybe overalls were the wrong choice. Eh, fuck it. It's not a date!*

If I knew then that I would eventually end up marrying this man, I might have paid closer attention to some of the hints to his personality traits that would one day drive me batshit crazy. For instance, I might have noticed that he was huffing and puffing from running twenty blocks uptown because he was too stingy to pay for subway fare. (Cheap bastard.) When I commented that his green jacket made it easy to find him, he bragged that he'd had that jacket since high school and had no intention of ever buying another one until he could afford a North Face, which wasn't really that expensive when you consider it as an investment for when he scaled Mt. Everest someday. (Cheap bastard mixed with label-whoreish ways and visions of grandeur.) The biggest warning, however, came during dinner. "I live with my parents," he stated proudly.

"What? You never told me that."

"It didn't come up."

"Because you're twenty-five. I didn't think it needed to 'come up.' I just assumed you lived on your own."

"Well, you know what they say about people who assume . . ."

"So, when will you move out?"

"I don't know. What's the rush? There's no rent, plenty of food, and my mom does my laundry."

"Ugh. Your mom still does your laundry? Can't you at least do your own laundry?"

"Why? She enjoys it."

"She doesn't enjoy it, you asshole."

"Whatever. Hey, check's here. Do you have exact change? I want to put it on my credit card so I can get the points toward my North Face."

After dinner Ebenezer offered to show me the sights of Manhattan. "I thought you weren't a tour guide," I teased him.

"I have a few places I could show you."

We walked around the city and he shyly took my hand, while *at the same time* he checked out the rack of some bimbo who walked by us. Yeah, like a full-on fucking head turn. I about broke his hand. "What? I've just never seen boobs that big on an Asian chick before," he said. "Do you think they were real?"

"I should get back," I said. I didn't want to buy my own dinner or compete with skanks with big boobs. I didn't care how much he made me laugh or how much fun we had together; it was disrespectful and I was tired of his assholey ways.

"Why?" he asked.

"Because you're being a dick. I don't even know why I came. I worked so hard to make this happen when you clearly did not care. So, I'm done. You're off the hook. You don't even need to walk me back to my hotel. I can get there on my own."

"Hold on," he said. "I'm sorry. I was just nervous, I think. I'm having fun with you and I want you to stay. I have something I want to show you. Will you hang out a little longer?"

"What do you want to show me?"

"It's a special place to me. It's close by. Come on." He grabbed my hand and pulled me toward Central Park.

At close to midnight.

As we walked deeper into the park, I finally asked, "Where are we going?" I tried not to let him know I was getting a bit nervous. My gut was telling me to knee him in the crotch and run.

"I told you I just finished shooting my first feature-length film, right?"

"Yes."

"Well, I want to show you where I filmed my favorite scene in the movie. It's just a little farther."

Finally we stopped on the path. "We're here," he said.

"I can't see anything," I said.

"Well, right through those weeds and stuff is the pond. The pond is my favorite spot in the whole park. Let's get closer—you can hear frogs."

All I could think was, *Are you fucking kidding me? You want me to get closer to the pond? Shit, I* am *going to end up on* Date-line. (I just want to go on the record right here that if my daughter ever does something this stupid, I'll kill her myself.)

"I've heard frogs before. I'm from Kansas," I said.

"Yeah, but the water is so pretty in the moonlight. Come on." He tugged on my hand.

Red flags, flashing alarms, code blue—all of it was going off in my head.

"Stop it!" I yelled. "Let go of me!"

"What's wrong, Jen?" Ebenezer asked, genuinely confused.

"You can't kill me! I won't go down without a fight, and if I can't stop you, I'll at least hurt you!"

"Holy shit, what is your problem? Why would you think I want to kill you? You're insane!"

"*I'm* insane? You're a stranger who brought me to the middle of a deserted park in the dead of the night, and you keep pushing me toward a pond so I can 'hear frogs'? I'm about ready to scratch out your eyes."

Ebenezer took five steps back from me. "Okay, settle down," he said holding up his hands in surrender.

"I want to leave. Now," I hissed.

"Okay. Let's go."

We walked in silence for a bit until my heartbeat slowed down and I determined Ebenezer was not going to kill me and dump my body in the pond. (By the way, this would be the first of many, many times I was convinced the Hubs was trying to kill me. In his defense, I bring out that instinct in many people, so he's forgiven.)

"I'm sorry," I said.

"It's fine. I didn't think that one through. I just wanted to share that place with you. Want some ice cream?"

"Yes, please!" Because ice cream always solves everything.

When he dropped me off at the hotel that night, he didn't even try to kiss me. I was positive he was still thinking about the fact that I'd threatened to scratch his eyes out less than an hour before. A little while later he called my hotel room.

"Hello?" I whispered, trying not to wake up C.B., who was in the next bed.

"What are you wearing?" he asked.

"Fuck you," I said. "Pajama overalls."

He laughed. "I had fun tonight."

"Me too," I admitted.

"I've got a problem, though."

"What's the matter?" I asked him.

"I'm woozy," he said.

"Well then, sit down! Put your head between your knees—"

"Hey, dummy, I'm woozy, because of you. *You* made me woozy tonight. I knew this was going to happen if we met."

"Oh," I said stupidly. I had no idea how to respond. All of my life boys and men have played games with me. I've always had to guess: *Does he* like *like me or does he just like me? Is he flirting with me or is he being nice?* I'd never had anyone be so frank about his feelings. "That's nice," I said, like an idiot.

"Yes. It *is* nice. So . . . you want to talk about *Star Wars* some more?"

Yes! Finally a topic I knew how to handle! "Okay."

After we'd spent an hour whispering on the phone, C.B. sat up, threw a pillow at me, and yelled, "You're an adorable Ewok and he's Luke Skywalker! Darth Vader is awesome and Leia is overrated! Fine. Whatever. Just please go to bed, you psycho!"

"I'll see you tomorrow," Ebenezer said.

And we hung up.

We've been together ever since, because I saw right through his gruff, dorky exterior and realized I'd be a complete fool to let this guy go. After all, there aren't too many men out there willing to put up with my brand of crazy.

Fifteen years later I know now that Ebenezer was afraid to meet me and that's why he was such an asshole. Don't get me wrong—he is a very blunt person with hardly any filter and couldn't tell a white lie if his life depended upon it (*never* ask this man if your butt looks big unless you can take the truth). He had a crush on me and knew I didn't feel the same way. He thought it was ridiculous to even meet, because it would just confirm his feelings and then he'd be stuck pining for a girl who lived in Kansas.

So there you have it: the most romantic love story you've ever heard. Basically we were two weirdos (future crazy cat lady Jen and parents'-basement-dweller Ebenezer) who found love chatting online in the Wild West days of the Internet when most people were creepers looking for cybersex.

For many years we were kind of ashamed to admit how we met, and whenever people would ask us, we'd always say, "A mutual friend."

We just never said our mutual friend was AOL.

TAKE YOUR MOTHER'S SANDWICH
AND SHOVE IT

I think every woman wonders at some point in her marriage, *Who the hell am I married to?*

The difference is, I wondered this on the morning of my wedding.

After several years of dating, the Hubs finally popped the question. In those days we were living in his hometown, New York City. Once I had the ring on my finger, I let him know that I'd had a good run in the big city. I'd put in five years, but I was tired of rubbing up against strangers' junk on the subway and fighting off vermin for the last loaf of bread at the grocery store. I was dreaming of more square footage, drive-through every-things, and a yard that someone else would mow. I convinced him we should move to the suburbs of Kansas, buy a McMansion, and raise our future kids in a planned community just down the street from my parents . . . and my brother . . . and my grandparents . . . and my aunts and uncles . . . and my cousins. I still can't believe he agreed to do it. But he did. We bought our first house in suburban Kansas one month before our wedding.

When our wedding day arrived it dawned overcast and

slightly dreary. Many of the older women in my family assured me that a rainy wedding day is a "lucky" wedding day. *Uh-huh. Sure it is.*

I tried to go about my pre-wedding details and not worry too much about the dismal weather and the havoc it would wreak on my hair. I went to my hair appointment that morning and paid a professional handsomely to flat-iron the shit out of my mane. I had her firmly attach my veil and spray the whole mess with shellac so as to prevent as many frizzies as possible. Then I headed to my parents' house to finish getting ready.

I was going to put on my dress at the church, but I wanted to do my makeup (following directions I carefully copied down from a *Mademoiselle* magazine for "dramatic eyes") under normal lights rather than the sickly fluorescents that church bathrooms are famous for. I also wanted to get together my last-minute "emergency kit" items (based on a list I carefully copied from *Bride* magazine), like Band-Aids (because you might cut yourself when you least expect it), drinking straws (so you won't smudge your lipstick), and a needle and thread (seriously, though, if it gets to the point that I'm going to be forced to sew something, then we've got major problems and maybe we should just consider postponing the wedding rather than letting me sew anything).

The last thing on my list was my ring bearer's pillow. A few months earlier I'd found a pattern for a really simple and elegant pillow. My aunt Ruby made the pillow for me and gave it to me at my bridal shower. It was so beautiful. It matched the patterned skirts that my bridesmaids wore, and I imagined it sitting on my (blissfully happy) marital bed for the rest of my life. I imagined my children someday resting their sweet little heads on my adorable pillow and asking me to tell them the story (again,

again!) of my romantic wedding, and how someday my daughter could use it at her wedding if she wanted. It would be an *heirloom.*

As I drove to my parents' house I started to wonder where exactly that damn pillow was. I know, I know—a more organized bride might have thought about this pillow weeks ago, but I think by now we've established that organization is not a skill I possess. Not even on my wedding day. I realized I hadn't seen the pillow since my bridal shower several months before. I was fairly certain it was in the shopping bag of assorted wedding odds and ends that I'd carted over to my parents' house the night before.

I was staying with my parents because I'm old-fashioned like that. The Hubs and I had purchased a house together earlier in the month, but he was staying there with his family and I didn't really want to be there taking care of them. I much preferred to stay with my parents and get spoiled a little bit.

When I got to my parents' house I immediately started digging through the shopping bag. The closer I got to the bottom without finding my pillow the more frantic I became.

"What's up?" my mom asked. "What are you looking for?"

"My ring bearer pillow. Have you seen it? I was sure I put it in this bag."

"You didn't. I was with you yesterday when you were packing that bag. You never grabbed the pillow."

"I didn't?"

"Nope."

"Hmm. Okay. Well, then it must be in the front hall closet at my house. Let me call Ebenezer and have him find it."

"Okay. I can run over and get it. That way he won't see you before this afternoon," my mom offered.

"Great. Thanks."

I grabbed the phone and dialed Ebenezer.

"Yup," he answered. He always answers "yup," and it drives me bonkers. How hard is it to say "Hello"? But there was no time to dwell on my betrothed's annoying habits—I had important business.

"It's me," I said.

"Yup."

"Listen, we have a problem. I can't find the ring bearer's pillow."

"Yup."

"Stop saying 'yup'!" I yelled. "This is important!"

"Well, what do you want me to do?" he asked impatiently.

"I need you to look in the front hall closet. On the top shelf there is a plastic grocery bag. Look inside there and tell me if the pillow is in there."

"I can't do that right now," he said. "I'm kind of busy."

Are you fucking kidding me? Who tells his bride on her wedding day that he's too busy to help her locate a very special and important item?

I took a deep breath. I didn't want to fight on my wedding day—we had a lifetime for that. "Well, *when* do you think you can look?" I asked as calmly as I could.

"I dunno. In a couple of hours."

"We have to be at the church in a couple of hours," I whispered, working extremely hard to control my emotions. I wanted to reach through the phone and strangle him. "I need you to look now, because if it isn't there, I have some other ideas where it could be."

"Why didn't you bring it to your mom's last night?" he asked.

"I thought I did. It didn't make it into the bag. That's why I need you to look. *Now.*"

"Yeah, well, like I said, I'm busy right now. It will have to wait awhile."

"What the hell are you doing that is so important?" I asked through gritted teeth.

"I'm making my mother a sandwich," he replied.

I held my breath and willed the blood vessel throbbing in my temple not to explode. I waited for him to tell me that his mother was in some kind of low-blood-sugar coma and needed a sandwich right away in order to live. I waited for him to tell me that in addition to her low-blood-sugar coma, she had fallen down the stairs and broken both of her arms and both of her legs and so she could not possibly make that lifesaving sandwich for herself.

"She's hungry and she won't be able to eat again until the reception later tonight. It's a big day for her, too, and she needs some food before we leave for the church."

"Mm-hmm," was all I could manage before I hung up the phone and started screaming. "Motherfucker!"

My mother came running. "What's wrong?"

"He is making his mother a sandwich," I seethed, barely able to talk. "A fucking sandwich. I haven't even had breakfast, but God forbid his *mother* misses a meal!"

"Okay, okay," my mother soothed. "What did he say exactly?"

"He said he can't look for my pillow because he's too busy making his mother a sandwich!" I wailed. "He said it was a 'big day for her, too.' What am I doing? Who am I marrying? He's choosing his mother over me!"

"Calm down." My mom stroked my expensive hairdo. "Tell

me where you think the pillow is and I'll go over there and look for it."

I gave her a list of five or six potential spots where I shove important shit and then promptly forget about it.

"Jen, you know this is sort of your fault, too," my mom said.

"How do you figure that?"

"Well, it's the day of your wedding. You should have located this pillow long before now. You're not even sure where it is, and you're upset because Ebenezer won't drop everything and go look for it. *You* didn't keep track of your stuff."

"Who cares?" I cried. "He won't help me because he's too busy helping his *mother*! I am going to be his *wife* after today. Aren't you supposed to choose your wife over your mother?"

"Look, who knows what he's thinking? I'm just telling you, this is your fault, too. Now, I will go over there and find the pillow. In the meantime, you'll probably want to get out the flat iron. Your hair is a little . . . messed up."

I looked in the mirror and saw that my hair was all jacked up and my veil was askew. "Son of a bitch. He's going to ruin my pictures, too!"

"Fix your hair. I'll get the pillow and I'll meet you at the church."

I can't remember why my mom and dad were going to the church earlier than I was. Probably to set up something that I thought was very, very, very important and needed to be done before I got there. All I remember is they threw on their wedding clothes and headed over to my house to dig through my closets while my future husband made his mother a delicious ham and cheese sandwich.

After they'd been gone for a bit, my mother called me. "I'm

not finding it in any of the places you told me to look. Is there anyplace else you shove stuff?" she asked, clearly exasperated.

"I don't think so. Did you look in the plastic bag in the hall closet?"

"Yes."

"The hatbox in the storage room in the basement?"

"Yes."

"The shelf in the garage where I keep extra toilet paper and paper towels?"

"Yes."

"Under the guest room bed?"

"Yes."

"The trunk of Ebenezer's car?"

"Yes."

"Wow. I was sure it would be in one of those places! Those are all of my good spots. Where could it be?"

"I haven't looked in the master bedroom closet yet."

"*No!*" Ebenezer and I both shouted at the same time.

The master bedroom closet is where we keep our . . . *equipment.* It's where I hide that naughty box of goodies that must be destroyed before my mother comes over to clean out my belongings if I'm ever hit by a bus.

"I'll look there," I heard Ebenezer say.

"Well, *that* certainly got him off his butt," my mom said, surprised. "I haven't seen him move that quick since I got here."

I sighed. He *did* love me. Either that or he was terrified of what *his* mother would say when *my* mother passed out after finding our collection of "love enhancers."

Ebenezer and my mother turned that house upside down and never did find that pillow. I cried for about an hour, ruining my gorgeous *Mademoiselle*-inspired makeup. My dramatic eyes now looked like something the editors might call "homeless person chic."

Aunt Ruby arrived to pick me up to take me to the church and was shocked to see me in such a mess.

"I lost your pillow!" I sobbed hysterically.

Aunt Ruby wiped the (obviously mislabeled) waterproof mascara from under my eyes and dried my tears. She jammed my veil back into my crispy hair and smoothed it down for me.

"Who cares?" she said. "It's just a pillow. It's no big deal."

"He made his mother a sandwich," I whispered.

"What?" Aunt Ruby asked.

"His mother. He made her a sandwich instead of looking for my pillow."

"But you're the one who lost it," Aunt Ruby said.

"Yes, but—"

Aunt Ruby cut me off. "Today you are marrying your best friend and the love of your life. You need to let the sandwich thing go."

"What about the pillow? What will the ring bearer carry?" I whined, pulling a tissue from my wedding emergency kit.

Aunt Ruby looked around. It was the end of October, and my mother takes holiday decorating very seriously. Christmas may be her favorite, but Halloween is a close second, and the house was brimming with fall decor. "What about this pumpkin?" she asked, plucking a small gray metal pumpkin with a handle from a sea of ghosts and goblins. "He'll look adorable with a pumpkin. Everyone will love it!"

Aunt Ruby was right. Everyone thought the pumpkin bucket was the cutest thing they'd ever seen.

When I finally got a chance to be alone with Ebenezer, I

couldn't resist letting him know how much it bothered me that he'd chosen his mother over me. "How was your mother's sandwich?" I asked him later that night on the dance floor.

"I never got it made. I had to go and hide your naughty toy box from your mother."

I wasn't making a horrible mistake marrying him. He chose me and my vibrator over his mother and her sandwich.

THE HUBS OR THE CLEANING LADY—
DON'T MAKE ME CHOOSE

I love my cleaning lady just a little bit more than I love the Hubs. No, that's not true. I love her a lot more than I love the Hubs, and I'm not afraid to tell her, or him.

Neither the Hubs nor I is a terrific housekeeper, so our first six months of wedded bliss were not very blissful. We didn't have much practice in the co-homeowning cleaning routine. We spent a stupid amount of time arguing over whose turn it was to sweep the kitchen or clean the toilets. After fighting for weeks and watching our house dive-bomb into a dusty death spiral, we knew we had to take action.

I decided to do what my mother did when I was a kid and didn't want to clean the house. I made up a chore chart. I divided up all of the cleaning responsibilities, and every week each of us would have new jobs to do around the house. I tried to be fair. For instance, one week I'd clean the toilets and he'd mop the floors. The following week he'd clean the toilets and I'd mop the floors. I tried to spread the "good" jobs and the "bad" jobs around as evenly as possible.

The chart worked for the first week—the week I was the one

assigned to scrub the toilets. But, of course, when the next week came and it was his turn to polish the thrones, the Hubs announced he didn't like my chart. He argued that he didn't have much "experience" cleaning toilets or mopping floors (as if I'd put myself through college working as a janitor or something) and didn't think he'd do a very good job. Rather than do a shitty job on the toilets twice a month, he thought *I* should clean the toilets and mop the floors every week while he focused on his natural talents: taking out the trash and running the vacuum on an as-needed basis.

As you might imagine, that conversation didn't go very well. I think it ended with me saying to the love of my life something along the lines of: "Go fuck yourself, Hubs. I'm sorry you're such a delicate flower, but I'm not built for domesticity any more than you are."

After that lively debate, we decided the chore chart was never going to work. But we had to do something. The situation was becoming desperate. The floor of our bedroom was rapidly disappearing under piles of laundry, I found myself contemplating buying new dishes just to avoid washing the ones in the sink, and I had stopped using the master bathroom because the Hubs refused to take my advice to sit to pee.

Our constant fighting was quickly getting out of control, and we were starting to throw around the phrase "marriage counseling." I've always thought marriage counseling and renewing your vows are the kisses of death for a marriage. You rarely see a couple come through counseling unscathed. It can't be good for your marriage to sit in a drab office in the middle of a lifeless strip mall telling a stranger that cleaning toilets is a blow to your masculinity. And don't even get me started on the vow renewals! It started with celebrities. There would be an item in the tabloids hinting about trouble in paradise, and suddenly they're doing a ten-page photo spread in *People* magazine showcasing their romantic and inspiring vow renewals on some Hawaiian island. Six months later, they're back on the magazine cover because—surprise!—they're getting divorced. This phenomenon is now creeping down into the peasantry. I've seen several of my friends plan elaborate, bank-breaking vow renewals in the tropics. Then we find out a few months later that he's been a serial cheater since they got married. He'd promised to change his ways, and renewing their vows was supposed to make him monogamous. Long story short, you will never hear about me and the Hubs renewing our vows. We're both too cheap to spring for a shindig like that when the possibility of divorce attorneys is on the horizon. We'd rather save our money so there will be more to fight over.

Anyhoo, now you can imagine my fear when marriage counseling was suggested. I was terrified. We were only six months into our marriage and already we were looking at bringing in the equivalent of hospice for our marriage. Something had to change, but what? One particular messy, angry day it hit me like a ton of bricks. We didn't need a chore chart or marriage counseling. What we needed was a cleaning lady!

When the Hubs agreed to move to Kansas from New York City, one of the conditions he negotiated was a lawn service. Spending his Saturday afternoons mowing the lawn and trimming bushes sounded like a nightmare to him. Plus, he really sucked at that sort of thing. If we let him take charge, our lawn would be all crabgrass and patches of dirt. With the Hubs on mower patrol, we'd never get a note from the homeowners' association telling us our grass was too long, but we might get some notes asking us to re-sod the whole yard, because it was such a damn pit. Having the lawn guy freed up the Hubs' schedule for some much needed nap time and kept our lawn lush and beautiful.

A cleaning lady could go into the same category as the lawn guy. Between the two of them, we could save our marriage!

I was worried, though. Cleaning ladies aren't cheap, and the Hubs hates to part with his money. I would have to tread lightly if I wanted to do this right.

That night when the Hubs got home from work I said to myself, *Be smooth, Jen.* Then I blurted out, "We're on the brink of ruin! Our marriage is in trouble and unless you want to get divorced before our one-year anniversary we need to hire a cleaning lady. Soon. Like this week!"

The Hubs thought about it for half a second before he said, "You know what? You're right. Okay. Let's do it." We take our marriage vows very seriously, and we'll do what it takes to keep the spark alive, even if it means hiring people to do the labor we have no desire (or skill set) to do. "It makes sense, Jen. We don't try to fix our furnace when it goes out—we call a pro. We don't change the brakes on the car—we call a pro. When we need our house cleaned, it just makes sense to hire a pro."

And just like that, the decision was made. Now I had to find someone. I wasn't sure how to go about the process. I looked at Craigslist, but those people could be serial killers for all I knew. I couldn't trust an online ad. I needed a referral from someone.

The first place I asked was at the neighborhood pool. I thought it would be a good place to start. I knew that lots of the neighbors had cleaning ladies. I had seen them show up during the week hauling their mops and brooms out of hatchbacks. I approached a group of women sunning themselves by the baby pool, and I asked, "Hi there! I was wondering, do any of you have a cleaning lady you could recommend?"

Brandy sat up on her lounge chair and said, "We've had our maid for twelve years and she's fabulous. She's like part of the family." *Ugh.* Of course she calls her cleaning lady a maid.

"I'm not really interested in a *maid.* I just want a lady who will come a couple of times a month to clean," I said.

"I understand, Jen. My maid only comes a couple of times a month."

"Oh, I just thought since you called her a 'maid' that she lived with you, like Alice on *The Brady Bunch* or something."

"God, no. I would never want Martina to live with me."

"But it sounds like you like her. Can I get her number?"

"Oh, sorry. Martina only works for me and my stepmother. We all prefer it that way."

"Oh. So you don't have a recommendation for me. Your . . . maid . . . has enough clients."

"Yes, that's true. I was just letting you know how invaluable a maid is. I hope you find a good one."

"Thanks."

Teri chimed in from the seat next to her, "Well, I can tell you who *not* to hire! I've been through ten housekeepers in six years. I am *so* picky when it comes to housekeepers. None of them clean my house as well I clean it myself. It's infuriating to look behind my washer and dryer and see dust bunnies. How hard is it to pull them out once a week and vacuum back there?"

"You're supposed to vacuum behind your washer and dryer?" I asked. Shit. Those tasks weren't even on my chore chart!

"Jen, when you get lint and dust collecting back there, it's a major fire hazard! You probably don't pull out your fridge, either, do you?"

She took one look at the utter confusion on my face and waved me away impatiently. "Actually, you'd probably be just fine with any of the ten I've fired. It doesn't sound as if you care that much about your house. If you want their numbers, call me tonight and I'll give them to you."

Lynn, who was floating on a raft in the baby pool, said, "You don't even have kids. Why do you need a cleaning lady? Kids are the ones who make a mess. It seems strange that you need a cleaning lady."

"Well, we both work," I said, trying to make that my excuse.

"Don't you work from home?" she asked.

"Yes . . ."

"You just need a system. Every day take a one-hour break from your work to do something around the house. Have your husband do it, too. Between the two of you working two hours a day, your house should sparkle!"

"Yeah, it's just that I sort of hate systems, and we'd prefer to pay someone who is good at cleaning and stuff."

"Well, I can't imagine having a stranger clean your house," said Cindy, joining the conversation. "It's like having a stranger raise your children. That's your house. It's your mess. How embarrassing for some woman to come into your private, personal space and have to clean up your filth."

"Okay, then. Thanks, ladies, I'm going to check Craigslist and take my chances with the serial-killer cleaning ladies."

After a little more asking around, I found Rosa. In order to afford her, the Hubs and I vowed to forgo travel and entertainment and only eat out at restaurants with buy-one-get-one-free coupons and dollar menus. It was a small price to pay to quit yelling at the Hubs and see my bedroom floor again.

Rosa was wonderful. Not only did this woman clean my toilets and mop my sticky kitchen floor, she wasn't afraid of any dirty job. One day I was sobbing over brand-new baby Gomer. I was trying to breast-feed him and I couldn't get him to latch on. He and I were both crying hysterically. Rosa came to see what all the noise was about. "I think I have to call my La Leche League mentor," I sobbed. "I need some tips to get him to latch on."

"It's okay," Rosa soothed me and Gomer. "I don't know what La Leche League is, but I'm here. I can help you. You need to take off your top. It's better to just be . . ." She struggled to find the right word. "No shirt to do this."

"Topless?" I asked.

"Yes. No top. It just gets in the way and makes the baby hot. Take it off."

I agreed reluctantly. Before I could protest too much, she whisked off my shirt, and then Rosa—the mother of eight—dropped her mop, rolled up her sleeves, grabbed my boob, shoved it in Gomer's mouth, and helped me feed him. She sat there for half an hour supervising and giving both of us encouragement. My beds didn't get changed that day, but she earned her money.

A few years ago Rosa gave us the scare of our lives. She called and told me she was taking an extended trip to visit family in Mexico. This wasn't unusual. She does this a couple of times a year. She goes by herself to visit her mother and leaves her husband in charge of the kids. She gave me a date five weeks in the future when she would be able to come to my house. I marked my calendar and then watched the dust bunnies pile up in the corners of the living room.

When the eve of Rosa's return was finally upon us, I started the frantic rushing around that's called "cleaning for the cleaning lady." You've got to clear the mail off the kitchen counter, put away the piles of shoes that have multiplied by the doors, throw the dirty clothes in the hamper, and make sure every damn itty-bitty Lego and Barbie shoe is off the floor, because the vacuum is merciless. That night I was freaking out, because Gomer's room wasn't ready, I had to write contracts for some of my real estate clients, and my Pinterest account was in terrible shape and was begging to be updated. Before I made myself crazy, I decided to call Rosa and just make sure she was really back in the country and planning to come the next day. Like I said, my Pinterest account needed some serious attention, and if I could focus on that and put off cleaning for the cleaning lady until tomorrow night . . .

I called her and got her voicemail. I left her a message: "Hey, Rosa, it's me, Jen. I hope you had a great time in Mexico. I was just wondering if you're still coming tomorrow. If you can't, it's no big deal, I just wanted to make sure . . ." *Because I'd rather read a book tonight than pick up tiny Legos off Gomer's floor.* "So, y'know. Just call me and let me know what your plan is. Thanks."

I decided to take a break at that point, because I'd picked up a bunch of shoes and made a phone call to Rosa. Surely those tasks had earned me a break. A few hours later I still hadn't done much except organize my Pinterest boards and try on summer clothes (if I'm cleaning up, I might as well clean out my closet, right?) and I still hadn't heard from Rosa. It was starting to get late, and if I was going to finish cleaning for the cleaning lady, I needed to do it in the next hour or so before I went to bed. I tried her again, and she answered. "Hello?"

"Oh! Rosa, you're there. How was your trip?"

"Hi, Jen. It was good. I'm glad to be back."

"I bet. So, are you coming over tomorrow, then? I'm trying to get ready, but I don't know if I'm going to make it. It's been such a busy night," I lied.

"Oh. Yeah. No, I'm not coming tomorrow."

I'm not going to lie. I was a bit relieved. I could finish organizing my closet now. "Okay. Maybe Saturday, then, or Sunday?"

"No, I don't think that will work, either."

I was perplexed. Saturday or Sunday always worked. "Okay. Well, what do you think? What have you got open?"

"Hmm . . . well . . . nothing. I moved."

Shut the fuck up. I had to sit down. I was feeling dizzy. "You what? You moved?"

"Well, my husband moved. So I moved, too. I came home from Mexico yesterday and he and the kids had moved to St. Louis. He put the kids in school and everything."

Seriously. Shut the fuck up. "St. Louis?"

"Yeah. He called me and said, 'Come here and live here with us in St. Louis.' So I did."

"St. Louis?"

"Yes. Have you heard of it?"

"*St. Louis?*"

"Yes."

Shut. The. Fuck. Up. I felt nauseated. "Yeah, I've heard of it. I'm just shocked that you're gone. I mean. Wow. Because I was planning on seeing you tomorrow."

"I know. But I live in St. Louis now. Javier got a job in St. Louis and the kids are in school here, and I can't stay in Kansas City alone."

"Yes. Yes. Of course you need to be with your family."

"I know. And my family is in—"

"St. Louis," I finished.

"Yes. It is nice here."

"Uh-huh. That's good to hear. Well, I don't know what to say except good luck, Rosa. Bye."

"Bye, Jen."

I hung up the phone with mixed emotions:

1. I got a reprieve. I could get back to my Pinterest boards and forget about Gomer's room.
2. Crap, I needed to find another cleaning lady, stat. Maybe this time I'd find one who cleans behind the fridge, because ever since my conversation with Teri, the thought of what was back there had been weighing heavily on me. I mean, not heavily enough for me to pull out the fridge myself and clean behind it, but heavily nonetheless.
3. WTF, Rosa? You've cleaned our house for eight years— when were you going to tell me you moved to fucking St. Louis and couldn't come *tomorrow*, when we were expecting you?
4. Shit, now my marriage would be in trouble. Rosa had single-handedly saved us from marriage counseling. There were kids in the mix now, and I couldn't take any chances.
5. Was she lying to me, because my house was such a pain for her to clean and she was trying to let me down easy?

When I told the Hubs about Rosa, he immediately went to number five on my list. "Nice job, Jen. You ran her off," he said.

"Me?"

"Yes, you. You never do a good enough job cleaning up for her, and it makes more work for her. And I heard you ask her last time she was here if she ever vacuums behind the dryer."

"Well . . ."

"That was probably the straw that broke her back."

"Shit. So you don't think she's in St. Louis?"

"No way. Call Marci and ask if she dumped them, too."

"I can't. What if Marci has no idea what I'm talking about? Then she'll know Rosa fired us. I'll be so embarrassed."

"You *should* be embarrassed. After all these years, Rosa had enough of you. She fired us. Now what are we going to do?"

"I don't know. I'll have to find someone else. Maybe Teri can give me that list of the ones she fired."

"Well, you better do something fast. I don't want to go to marriage counseling."

I spent the next couple of weeks searching for a new cleaning lady. I couldn't find anyone who clicked with me like Rosa did. Even though I was long past my breast-feeding days, every time I interviewed a potential candidate all I could think was, "Would I let this woman grab my naked boob?"

I was starting to get worried—I'd even created a board on Pinterest I called "Marriage Vow Renewal Ideas"—when one day my phone rang. "Hello?" I answered.

"Jen?" a familiar voice asked.

"Rosa?"

"Yes, it's me, Jen. How are you?"

"I'm not good, Rosa. How are you?"

"I'm not good, either. I miss you."

"I miss you, too."

"I hate St. Louis."

"Oh. So you *really did* move there?"

"Of course I did, Jen. Did you think I didn't?"

"It doesn't matter now, Rosa. You were saying you hate St. Louis. . . ."

"Yes. And the kids hate St. Louis."

"Oh." I felt a little tingle. If Rosa hates it *and* the kids hate it, maybe . . .

"Javier hates St. Louis."

Yes! I tried to play it cool. She'd hurt me, but I didn't want her to know. "Oh."

"I come Saturday, Jen?"

Oh please God, yes. "Saturday would work for me, Rosa."

"I can clean behind the fridge now. I know you like that."

"No!" I cried. I'd just gotten her back—I didn't want to rock the boat with outrageous demands and risk losing her again. "We'll just stick with your usual routine, Rosa. Just do what you do best."

"Okay, Jen. I see you Saturday."

"Rosa . . ."

"Yes, Jen?"

I hesitated. Could I really say it? How could I not say it? I had lost her and now she was back. Had I learned nothing from all of those "Can This Marriage Be Saved?" articles I'd been using as makeshift marriage counseling for the Hubs and me during her absence? Rule number one: tell your loved one what they mean to you—out loud and often. "Rosa, I love you."

"I know, Jen."

GOD BLESS AMERICA (AND THONGS)

With our cleaning lady situation locked down and our marital bliss revived, the Hubs and I headed into our first summer in Kansas. I'd recently started a new job at a large company selling office equipment. We didn't know too many people who weren't related to me, and we were looking to branch out and meet some new people, so when Maryanne, a woman in my office, invited us to her Fourth of July party, I accepted.

"Remind me again: how do you know this woman?" the Hubs asked as he drove to Maryanne's house and I balanced a tray of deviled eggs on my lap.

"We work together. She's in the cubicle next to me. I can always hear her on the phone wheeling and dealing. She has a lot of big accounts. It seems like every day she's selling truckloads of Aeron chairs while I'm struggling to get my clients to pull the trigger on a box of staples."

"Hmm. Okay. And you're sure we can see the fireworks from her house?" The Hubs is a bit of a pyromaniac.

"Yes," I sighed. "Maryanne lives in the neighborhood right next to the park where they shoot off the fireworks. She told me we can see them easily from her backyard. It will be so nice not to have to deal with all the crowds at the park!"

"Good, because I want to see the fireworks."

"I know." I sighed again. *God, can he be any more demanding?* I didn't know it then, but he was actually training me on how to deal with our future children someday.

"And why did we need to get this dressed up?" the Hubs asked, tugging on his "good" (aka clean) shorts, which I'd made him put on.

"You're not even that dressed up! You're wearing a pair of shorts that required a bit of ironing. Relax. I'm the one in a dress! I just wanted us to look nice. Maryanne is very professional and she would be a great mentor for me at the office. I need to suck up to her a bit. I have no idea what her friends will be like, but just once in my life I would like to make a good first impression. My mother taught me that you can never be overdressed, but you can be *under*dressed."

We rang the doorbell and a woman with bright red hair wearing the tiniest star-spangled bikini I've ever seen up close and personal answered the door. Sure, you see those types of bathing suits in *Sports Illustrated* or something, but they're almost always on toned, tanned, perfectly styled, and airbrushed twentysomething models. This one was tied around a fifty-year-old piece of rawhide that had been left out too long in the sun. The only thing that didn't sag on her body was her boobs. Her huge fake breasts looked like small beach balls glued to her chest. *Holy crap!*

"Maryanne?" I asked cautiously. Maybe Maryanne was on the phone closing a hot deal on an all-in-one scanner copier fax machine and this was her sister, whom she'd just picked up from the plastic surgeon's office.

"Joslyn!" Maryanne slurred, enveloping me in a bear hug. "Of course it's me!"

I choked on the fumes emanating from her. It was a combination of coconut tanning oil, Jell-O shots, and body odor. "It's Jen, actually," I corrected her.

"Right! Jen. So glad you could come! Come on in and meet the gang. You're so late!"

"Well, you said we should come anytime. We wanted to come in time to see the fireworks."

"Cool. That makes sense. Well, you missed a helluva day. We've just been playing in the pool and drinking and doing Jell-O shots and having a lot of fun. I'm sorry you missed it. But you know what? You're here now. And now you can play! Did you bring a swimsuit?" she asked, looking me up and down.

"No. You didn't mention you had a pool."

"I didn't? Oh well, yeah, I do. And a hot tub!"

"It's okay, I don't really like to wear a swimsuit."

"I hear ya! You guys can totally skinny-dip. You won't be the first naked butts in my pool!" she cackled.

"I can't swim!" the Hubs said quickly. It was a half-truth. The Hubs is a terrible swimmer.

"Ah, whatever! Come on in!" Maryanne ushered us through her immaculate house, where professional family photos hung on the walls. A picture of Maryanne and three teenagers, all subtly color-coordinated and posing in a wheat field, hung over the sofa. Another picture of Maryanne and the three teenagers playfully frolicking together in jeans and white T-shirts hung over the piano. In the kitchen a huge photo magnet dominated the refrigerator. This one was Maryanne in her signature red power suit leaning casually against our company's most popular color copier. When I saw that one I nudged the Hubs and whispered, "That's the real Maryanne!"

"Sorry, Jen, but I think *this* might be the real Maryanne," he whispered back, pointing at Maryanne's tanned derriere hanging out of her thong. *My eyes! Her swimsuit is a thong!*

"Look who I found!" Maryanne called as we stepped out onto the patio. "It's Joslyn and her hubby!"

A chorus of hellos rose up. I looked around the pool to see who was there. I'd heard Maryanne inviting many people from the office, and I was sure there would be someone I would recognize. But I didn't see one face that I knew. *Where is everyone? I wondered. And who the hell are these people?*

We were surrounded by more fiftysomething people in teeny-tiny patriotic swimwear. WTF?

"Hi there," a barrel-chested man in extra-small flag shorts said, smiling at me.

"Hello," I replied.

"Want to try the hot tub? It feels great today!"

"Uh . . . no thank you." I looked around for the Hubs. Surely he would not like this semi-nude man chatting up his new wife. I couldn't see him anywhere.

"Maryanne said you forgot your suit," Flag Shorts went on. "It's okay, Elliot forgot his suit, too!" He pointed to a bald man lounging luxuriously in the hot tub.

"I always 'forget' it!" Elliot laughed.

"You're so bad!" Maryanne squealed as she jumped into the tub next to Elliot. Before I could avert my eyes, they started making out full throttle.

"My eggs," I squeaked. "I need to get them out of the heat before they spoil. Excuse me."

I turned back toward the house and heard Elliot call, "Hey, Joslyn, after you put those down, come on back! I'll save you a seat! Maryanne doesn't mind sharing, do you, babe?"

"Nope. I'll share if Joslyn will share," Maryanne said.

Are you fucking kidding me? Holy shit! This was no ordinary Fourth of July party with co-workers. These people were swingers! And not hot ones. God, why are swingers always so gross? Why is it always old, fat men with ponytails and wrinkled women with fake boobs? Why can't I just once be invited to a swingers party where I'm the hideous one and everyone else is smoking hot? It's a pretty sad state when *I'm* the best-looking one at the swingers party!

I ran into the house and quickly found the Hubs hoovering appetizers off the food table. "They're swingers! They're swingers! Red alert! They want to have sex with us!" I grabbed the Hubs' plate and threw it in the trash. "Stop eating their food! We can't owe them anything. We cannot be in their debt. They will want to be paid in blow jobs!"

"What the hell are you talking about, Jen?" the Hubs asked, starting another plate of food.

"Put down the food and listen to me! I just got invited into a threesome with Maryanne and some old douchebag who isn't wearing a swimsuit!"

"You did? Is there anyone good for me?" the Hubs teased me.

"Shut up. This is serious. We need to go! These people might rape us!"

"No one is going to rape us. They're too old and too drunk. We can totally fight them off. Besides, this pasta salad is delicious. I'm not leaving until you try it." He offered me a forkful of pasta.

"I'm being serious!"

"So am I. This is fantastic! Is the grill hot out there? I want to grill up one of these brats."

"Oh my God! Don't go out there! They'll invite you into the hot tub."

"Relax, Jen. I just want to make a brat."

"Seriously, stop eating right now! I want to leave. I am *very* uncomfortable with this."

"Hold on. *You* are the one who wanted to come here. You told me that Maryanne is so cool and you wanted her to be your mentor. You wanted a mentor, so get mentored. I'm going to eat. Where are your eggs?"

"You're really going to eat?"

"Of course. I'm starving. I didn't eat much lunch, because I hoped there would be a spread like this. Just grab a seat on the couch and wait a few minutes for me."

I sat on the couch gazing at Maryanne's normal-looking family pictures while the Hubs stuffed his face. *Where are her kids today?* I wondered. *Do they know their mother is a swinger?*

"Joslyn?" It was Flag Shorts. "Are you coming back outside? We've got Jell-O shots."

"Thanks, but I can't. My *husband* needs me to stay in here with him while he eats." I emphasized "husband," hoping Flag Shorts would get the hint.

"I can't borrow her for a bit?" Flag Shorts asked the Hubs.

The Hubs chewed his cud slowly and contemplated the question. *You son of a bitch!* "No," he finally said. "She's right. I need her with me. I like her to get my food for me. Joslyn, I need more deviled eggs, woman!"

Flag Shorts shrugged and left us.

"I will be in the car," I announced.

"Wait. I'm not done," the Hubs said.

"I don't care. I will be in the car. Waiting for you."

"What about Maryanne? Don't you want to say goodbye?"

"No. She doesn't even know my name. She's so sauced she won't even remember I was here."

I got out to the car and texted my co-worker Dennis.

Jen: Hey, what's the deal with Maryanne?

Dennis: Why? Did she invite you to her party?

Jen: Yes.

Dennis: DON'T go.

Jen: Too late.

Dennis: LOL. Is she in her thong?

Jen: Yes!

Dennis: Sorry. Thought you knew. She's tightly wound at work, so when she's home, she likes to let loose.

Jen: She likes to swing!

Dennis: Yeah, that too. You really didn't know?

Jen: Of course not.

Dennis: Thought everyone did. Every year she ropes some newbie into coming to her party. You're the sucker this year.

Jen: Great. You saw me talking to her; you should have told me.

Dennis: Sorry. Didn't you see the rock when you pulled up to her house?

Jen: What rock? What are you talking about?

Dennis: The white rock in the flower beds by her front door.

I looked up, and sure enough, there was a large white boulder nestled into her flowers.

Jen: I see it now. So what?

Dennis: Wow. You have a lot to learn about this town. Didn't your Realtor tell you? They all know that a white rock like that means you're a swinger. It lets other swingers know they're welcome. It's also a warning to those who don't swing. It lets them know to steer clear.

Jen: Oh shit.

Dennis: Well, now you're stuck.

Jen: No I'm not. I'm in the car. We're leaving.

Dennis: You can't leave.

Jen: What do you mean?

Dennis: Her neighborhood is shut down. The cops put up barricades to control the crowds for the fireworks. The barricades are up. You can't leave until the fireworks are over. You might as well go have a Jell-O shot and enjoy the display.

Jen: How do you know so much?

Dennis: Who do you think the sucker was when I was a newbie? Tell Elliot I said hello and that I would still like to buy him a swimsuit whenever he's ready. Happy Fourth of July! At least this will be one you'll never forget!

The Hubs joined me on the curb with a plate of food he'd made for me. He was right—the pasta salad *was* delicious. I showed him the text messages from Dennis. "We're trapped," I told him.

"Sounds like it."

"Where's the platter my eggs were on?" I asked him.

"I forgot it. I really don't want to go back in there. It's starting to get a little strange. I'll get you a new one."

"Okay."

We watched the fireworks alone from the street and then headed home.

On Monday my deviled egg platter was on my desk. It was sparkling clean and a Post-it was attached: JOSLYN.

JUST SOME OF THE MANY REASONS
THE NEIGHBORS ALWAYS HATE US

The Hubs and I have always had trouble making friends with our neighbors. We're not total curmudgeons who yell at the kids to keep off our lawn, but we do let it be known that we're never happy to find someone else's dog shit on our grass, and we rarely walk over someone's junk mail that was accidentally placed in our mailbox. I actually think that last one is very neighborly of us. Who really wants that mailer with the practically worthless coupons from the expensive dry cleaner? My neighbor should thank me for recycling it for him and then we can avoid the awkward chitchat about how I saw him watch his dog take a dump in my bushes last week.

We're not very good at the niceties and the small talk that are required to be a good neighbor, so block parties and barbecues tend to be awkward. Our politics rarely jibe (we're a couple of mouthy liberals living in the heart of red country), and we don't give a shit about sports, especially college basketball and hyper-competitive soccer for young children, which are the favorites around here.

When we first moved to Kansas City, we bought a house that

was a huge compromise. The Hubs wanted a house with lots of mature trees, but this was Kansas. Our neighborhood was a cornfield two years ago. Trees are expensive, and homes with trees weren't in our price range. We could afford bushes. I wanted something with character but not a fixer-upper. In the end we got a well-built beige cookie-cutter house without a tree in sight. It was in an area we liked and was close to my parents but not *too* close, it had a finished basement for the Hubs and his video games, and it had tons of beautiful landscaping for me to kill. It was in our price range and neither one of us hated it.

We met our next-door neighbors, Nicole and Matthew, right after we moved in. They seemed like people we could be friends with. Like us, they were young professionals and childless, which was rare in that neighborhood. We were surrounded by stay-at-home moms whose children kept multiplying. As much as I hoped we could be friends with Nicole and Matthew, it didn't take us long to piss them off. Although theirs was a child-free home, they did have a dog. A big, friendly yellow Lab named Daisy. About a month had gone by when we ran into Matthew and Daisy at the mailbox one evening. I noticed right away that the fur on Daisy's back leg had been shaved and she had an enormous scar running the length of her hindquarter.

"What happened to Daisy?" I asked.

"Oh, it was terrible," Matthew said. "She was chasing a rabbit and jumped off our deck and fractured her leg in several places."

"Oh wow. That *is* terrible," I said. "Looks like she had to have surgery."

"Yes, she did," Matthew said.

"Your dog had to have surgery?" the Hubs asked. "That doesn't sound cheap."

"It's actually a sore subject with Nicole. We had to pay thirteen thousand dollars for her surgery."

"You paid thirteen grand for a *dog* to have surgery?" the Hubs sputtered.

Matthew looked irritated. "Don't you guys have a dog?" he asked.

"No," the Hubs replied. "We're going to have kids."

"Well, you can have a dog *and* kids, you know. And if you don't have kids, your dog can be *like* your kid. No one would question this surgery if Daisy was our child. The Bonds—the family who lives behind us—they paid ten grand for braces for their kid, and that's just cosmetic. Daisy was never going to walk again without this surgery."

"Yeah, but she's a *dog*. The Bonds' kid is . . . y'know, a *kid*," the Hubs challenged.

I could tell that Matthew was getting pissed off at the Hubs. I didn't know what else to do, except dig our hole deeper. "So, Nicole wasn't happy about how much it cost?" I asked.

"No, she wanted to put Daisy down."

"Smart woman," the Hubs said.

"Look, man, I've had this dog longer than I've even *known* Nicole, okay? This dog is far more loyal and loving to me than my wife. If she needs surgery, I'll do whatever I have to do to get her what she needs."

"A few months ago Nicole was telling Jen that you guys are thinking of moving in a year or so and she wanted Jen to list the house. She told Jen you were saving for a kitchen remodel," the Hubs said.

"Yeah. We *were*. We had to use that money on Daisy. That's why Nicole is so pissed. She's so caught up in *stuff*. She doesn't give a damn about Daisy."

Never one to sugarcoat, the Hubs said, "Well, when you guys call Jen in to sell your house, I'm sure Nicole will be happy to remind you that your house would be worth about thirty thousand dollars more if you'd done the kitchen remodel instead of the surgery. Also? Daisy might be dead by then. She's pretty old." And there it was. The sentence that ruined any chance at friendship with these people.

When Matthew and Nicole put their house on the market a year later, I didn't get that listing—and Daisy was still alive.

After a few years and the birth of our first child, we decided it was time to find a house we loved. After our experience with Matthew and Nicole, I'd accepted the fact that the Hubs and I were never going to become besties with the family next door. We were never going to get together with our neighbors on nice evenings to drink cold beverages or while away the afternoon together at the neighborhood pool. It just wasn't going to happen for us. We're offensive and we know it and we can't help it. So we focused more on the house than the neighborhood. After a few weeks of hunting, we found it: unique (no cookie-cutter suburban house for us this time around), lots of trees and character, an open floor plan with four bedrooms and an eat-in kitchen on a cul-de-sac within a mile of a highly ranked elementary school and less than three miles from SuperTarget. Our own little slice of heaven!

We had just moved in when one of our new neighbors came over to welcome us to the 'hood. They brought their young children with them as well as a loaf of homemade banana bread. After exchanging pleasantries about the house ("Yes, we love it. Yes, we painted it, put in new flooring, and upgraded some of the light fixtures. You'll need to come in for a tour sometime once we're not living out of boxes anymore."), I was beginning to think maybe we'd put our bad-neighbor karma behind us. Maybe Matthew and Nicole were a fluke. Maybe the banana bread people would be different. I found myself imagining what it would be like to borrow a cup of sugar from these people or carpool to school someday. I let myself dream of a friendship that might be.

And then the wife asked, "Do you have children?"

"Yes. We have a baby boy. His name is Gomer. He's seven weeks old," I replied.

"Oh. How wonderful. You're just getting started!" the husband exclaimed.

"How old are your kids?" I asked.

"I'm four!" the little girl said loudly. Her parents smiled adoringly at her. (She *was* pretty darn cute.)

"Four is so big! Do you go to school?" I asked.

"Yes. I'm in preschool." Her parents beamed.

"Wow, that's impressive. You must be learning a lot," I said.

"Yes. I know all of my colors," she said proudly. Her parents swooned.

Don't get me wrong, I was—and still am—very much in love with Gomer, but this was too much.

"And what about you?" I asked her younger brother.

"I'm four, too!" he cried, holding up three fingers. The preciousness of it all was almost too much for his parents, who practically keeled over.

"Hmm . . . are you sure?" I teased him. "You're four, too?"

"Yup!" he said, overjoyed. Dad's chest just about burst open with pride.

"Well . . . if you say so," I said.

"Oh, buddy, you're so funny," his dad said. "Tell them how old you really are."

"I did! I'm four!" he said, stomping his little foot.

"Nooo," his mother said. "You're . . ." She waited for him to fill in the blank.

He just glared at her.

"I'm four! I'm four! I'm four!" he screamed.

My visions of carpooling dimmed. I wasn't so sure I wanted this kid in my car. He was becoming a bit obnoxious, and frankly, I was bored with him. I didn't give a shit how old he was. I wanted to go back inside and try the delicious-smelling banana bread without this kid ruining it.

"I said I'm four!"

"Okay, okay. If you say so, buddy," his dad said. He smiled knowingly at us. "Just you two wait until you get one like this. 'High-spirited' is the word his teachers at Moms' Day Out use. He's such a blessing, though. Oh, and he's really two."

"Ohhh," the Hubs said, crouching down to the boy's level. "I get it. You're not four. You're . . . a *liar*." The Hubs spat the word "liar" with so much vitriol and disdain, it was like he was a lawyer in a murder case accusing the defendant instead of a grown man talking to a two-year-old fibber.

Everyone was silent for a good thirty seconds while the little liar's parents stared in horror at the Hubs. *Maybe they'll laugh,* I thought. *Maybe they're really witty and they can see that the Hubs isn't an asshole, he's just a guy without a filter and the best way to shut him up is to laugh when he says stupid things.*

"He's not a liar. He's *two*," the dad hissed. "He doesn't know *how* to lie."

Nope. Not gonna happen. I kissed driveway happy hours and barbecues goodbye and realized I would need to make that banana bread last, because I was never going to get another loaf.

SCREW YOUR PLAYGROUP, I DIDN'T WANT TO JOIN ANYWAY

I was a work-at-home mom when my son, Gomer, was born. I had left my job selling office equipment to start my own real estate team. This decision was thanks partially to the Fourth of July swinger party fiasco. I just couldn't stop seeing Maryanne's itty-bitty bikini every time we passed each other in the hallway. I'd been working hard to build my own team for a few solid years before Gomer came along. So within weeks of his birth, I strapped on my BabyBjörn and hit the listings.

I was actually able to strike a great work-life balance. The Hubs hooked me up with a sweet home office and Wi-Fi so I could sit on my bed with a snoozing Gomer cuddled up against me and a laptop in my lap. If I had to show a house or two, I'd take Gomer in his infant carrier seat and leave him sleeping in the front hall of the house I was touring. (Don't worry, Nervous Nellies, I always made sure the front door was locked so no one could sneak in and snatch my adorable baby.)

Gomer was my little assistant. I would set him up on the floor with a few toys and he would play happily while I returned phone calls and emails. One of his favorite toys was a kiddie laptop and one of my old cell phones. As he got older, he would pretend to sell houses, too. He would "call" clients on his phone and say things like "Hello? Need house?" or "Joe [the name of my favorite lender], will we close? Will we?"

At first I thought this was hilarious. I thought my little toddler loved his mama so much that he wanted to be just like her. I had visions of him growing up and joining my real estate team. We'd be Jen & Son—House Hunters. Until the day I heard, "Hello? Joe? Wanna come play?"

"What did you ask Joe, Gomer?" I asked, hoping I had misheard him.

Gomer looked me with the saddest little eyes I'd ever seen. "Come play," he said.

I was a terrible, shitty mother. Here I thought I was doing the right thing by keeping him home with me, where he could be raised and nurtured by me, instead of sending him to day care, where he'd be just another cog in their machine of germy kids. In fact, I was screwing him up! He had no friends and he knew it. He understood that it wasn't normal to sit home all day with his mother and an old cell phone to keep him company. He was going to be that weird kid in kindergarten who wouldn't know how to play with his peers or share toys. I had to fix this. Fast.

I turned to the one place that never lets me down when I'm making big life decisions: the Internet. I searched for a local playgroup, and the first one that popped up sounded perfect. They had playgroups several days during the week and activities for just the moms at night. I forked over my credit card number without even attending a meeting.

The first meeting I could attend was the following week. I arrived a little early because I hate walking into a room full of strangers. I'd rather get there early and find a good dark corner where I can camp out and survey the land a bit before I venture out of my comfort zone.

The first person I met was the woman in charge of the playgroups. "Oh great! You're just the person I want to see," I exclaimed. "I have a two-year-old and he needs some friends."

"Great. We'd love to have you," she replied.

"I looked at the website and I saw that you're going to the fire station tomorrow. Gomer would love that. He really likes firemen," I blathered.

"Oh, I'm sorry, that won't be possible," she said, cutting me off. "That's the *Red* Group's activity. You'd be in the *Orange* Group. The Orange Group is going to a tour of the grocery store on Friday. You're welcome to join them then."

"Friday? Oh, I can't do Friday. I have a listing appointment on Friday. That's why I wanted to go to the fire station tomorrow, when my schedule is open."

"I don't think you're understanding. The Red Group is full. There is no more room in the Red Group. Only the Orange Group has room. They always meet on Fridays."

"Well, what's the difference? Do they do the same things?" I asked.

"There is no difference really. However, they don't do the same things." *Uh, I think that's a difference, lady.* She went on, "I personally arranged for the fire station visit because I'm good friends with someone in the department. I'm not sure the Orange Group could get a tour, since they don't know anyone there."

"So, you're in the Red Group?" I asked.

"Of course," she replied. "I told you, I planned the trip to the firehouse. Each group plans their own activities. Obviously someone in the Orange Group has a connection with the grocery store."

"But the Orange Group won't work for me. Fridays are typically busy days for me. I'm a Realtor"—I gave her my card; always be selling—"and most people like to list their houses on a Friday. So I like the group that meets on Wednesdays." Plus I didn't want to go take a tour of the damn grocery store! I was in there all the time. I wanted to see some hot firemen! I mean, I wanted Gomer to learn about fire safety.

"Sorry, but Wednesdays are the Red Group. And—"

"Yes, I know. It's full. Only the Orange Group has room," I finished. This chick was like a broken record.

How fucked up is that? I thought. *How can you have a playgroup that's "full"?*

"Hi, you must be Jen!" Another woman walked up to us. "I'm one of the co-presidents of the group. I saw your membership form come through. So nice to meet you. I'm glad you could join us."

"Yeah, hi. I'm not sure I can join," I replied. "I think I need a refund."

"That's fine. We can get that taken care of tonight," the playgroup lady said. "Did you pay by credit card or check?"

"Hold on!" the co-president said. "Why do you want a refund? What's the matter?"

"She says I can't be in the Red Group," I whined like a toddler. "There's only room in the Orange Group and they meet on Fridays, which is a terrible day for me, because I'm a Realtor—here's my card—and Fridays are the absolute worst day for me."

"I don't understand. Why can't she be in the Red Group?" the co-president asked the playgroup warden.

"It's full," she said.

"Full? I didn't realize our playgroups had limited spaces."

"They can and they do."

"I'm sorry, Jen, my kids are in school, so I'm not as involved in the playgroups as I used to be. I stick around for the Moms' Night Out stuff," the co-president said to me.

"You've known about this problem. We've discussed it at our board meetings," the playgroup warden said. (Yeah, they have a board of directors and shit. They're serious about their playgroups.) "I told you that the Wednesday playgroup is the most popular and several of our members have asked me to limit the number of members because their children become overstimulated."

"Oh, right, I sort of remember that now. Well, isn't there room for one more in the Red Group? Jen can't make the Orange Group work for her schedule."

"No, there isn't. If I make an exception for her, I'd have to make it for others."

"Maybe someone from the Red Group would move to Orange?" the co-president tried.

"*No one* would move from Red to Orange," the warden said, looking horrified.

She confirmed what I was thinking: overstimulated kids my ass, this was all about the "right kind" of moms. The Red Group was obviously the "cool moms." Suddenly I had no desire to be in the Red Group anymore.

"Just out of curiosity, how do you get to be in the Red Group?" I asked.

"It's based on seniority. There was an original group that typically met on Wednesdays, and then we've added just a few to our group over time as spaces have opened up. The moms pick who they would like to join and extend an invitation. It's just easier that way."

"How is that easier?" I asked.

"Because then they know exactly who will be joining their group, rather than some random person off the Internet."

"Like me."

"Well, it's true that we don't know you—or your son," she added, like he might be the problem.

Suddenly I felt compelled to defend Gomer. "He's vaccinated and he's not a biter or anything like that!"

"Oh, I'm sure he isn't. Just know that the Red Group really isn't a place for newcomers. We're very close, and even our husbands are close. It's a solid group. The Orange Group is a better fit for you," the warden explained.

"You know what? Never mind. I'm going to find something else for me and Gomer to do. We don't need to do this." I started fumbling with my purse to get my car keys so I could leave. I was furious. Who did this bitch think she was, telling me that her playgroup was full?

"Hold on," the co-president said. "Maybe we could start another Wednesday playgroup? Maybe there are enough people who would be interested in having another group? Would that be okay with you, Jen? Would you stay if I could find some people to do that?"

I stopped what I was doing and I listened to her. *She* wasn't so bad. She was actually trying to make it work, while the warden just kept saying no, no, no, no!

"I think that would be fine. I just want to find some friends for my son, and I'd prefer that it be on a Wednesday," I said.

"Great. No problem. I'll find some people."

"I'm not sure I have time for that—," the warden started.

The co-president cut her off. "Don't worry. I'll take care of it."
And she did.

Within a week I had a playgroup to attend with Gomer. I think we were called the Blue Group.

I was still so pissed off about the whole Red Group/Orange Group thing that I had a really hard time being nice to the warden anytime I saw her after that. It made me wonder how many other women in the group she'd treated like shit. I was lucky, because the co-president had been around to see what was happening and she took over, but I could only imagine how many times that same conversation went down in private without anyone reining in that control freak.

Why the fuck did she have to make it so damn difficult? All I wanted was to find my kid a friend to play with on a day of the week that worked best for me. What the hell? Was I getting caught up in the Mommy Wars I'd heard so much about? This was my first foray into the world of WAHMs and SAHMs. But then I realized it wasn't a Mommy War; I'd just come across a plain old bitchy mom.

Over the next couple of years I worked my way up the rungs of power until I was elected co-president of the group. Can you guess what my first order of business was? Yup—I axed the membership limits for the Red Group and the Orange Group and the Blue Group and any other playgroup I could find. I opened them all up to everyone.

After all, I didn't want a group going to meet hot firemen without me!

GOMER MIGHT BE A RACIST

When the Hubs agreed to move to suburbia with me, his biggest concern for our future children was diversity. Or rather, the lack thereof.

As I've mentioned before, the Hubs is Chinese and I am not, so our kids are biracial. The Hubs was worried that living in such a white-bread place, our kids could be victims of racism and bullying.

I had spent three long, hard years going to high school in this town, and I knew firsthand what he was afraid of. Because of that, I was always on high alert looking for Gomer and Adolpha to be discriminated against.

When Gomer was three, I opened up his peer circle beyond the Blue Playgroup and enrolled him in preschool. It was a peer modeling program where half the class were peers and the other half were kids with special needs. This type of classroom was supposed to teach him leadership skills, empathy, and understanding. I had visions of his days being filled with everyone sitting around singing "Kumbaya" and painting rainbows.

I noticed all was not right one day when I picked him up after school. Gomer has always been a child who loves to chat in the car. I find out the best stuff in the car. Sometimes I even go around the block just one more time so I can get to the end of a good story. That day was no different.

"How was school today?" I asked.

"It was okay," he sighed.

"Just okay? Why's that?"

"We didn't get enough time to play outside."

"Oh yeah? Recess is fun, huh?"

"Yeah, and this week we started a new game that we like. We didn't want to stop today."

"What game? Is it one that Ms. Rebecca made up?"

"No. It's one that Oscar made up. Ms. Rebecca doesn't even know we play it."

"How do you play?"

"Well, we are all good guys and we chase the big dark monster."

"Hmm, that sounds interesting. Why are you chasing the big dark monster?"

"Because he's bad. He's dark. And bad."

"I see. How do you decide who the big dark monster is?"

"Oh that's easy. It's always Sharu."

"What?" I felt myself jerk the steering wheel. Sharu was another peer model in the class. He was Indian and very dark-skinned. "What do you mean, he's always the dark monster?" I asked, trying to keep my voice from squeaking. *Oh my God! What the hell, Gomer?*

"Well, Oscar says Sharu has to always be the big dark monster because his skin is so dark."

The wheel jerked again and I almost drove off the road this time. *Shit! Are you kidding me?* By this time I was in our neighborhood, and I pulled to the curb, where I could park. I turned in my seat and faced what, up until now, I had always thought was my sweet, innocent, open-minded, unbiased child.

"Gomer, you can't always make Sharu the bad guy," I scolded him.

"But we have to. He's so *dark*," Gomer emphasized.

"Gomer! That is terrible. Tell me *exactly* how you play this game."

"Well, me and Oscar and Brice chase Sharu around the playground. We have to catch him and put him in jail. If he catches us first, though, he turns our skin dark and then we're bad guys."

My heart was racing. *Oh my God, oh my God, oh my God. WTF? The Hubs is going to kill me when he hears this. He'll make us move back to New York. I can't go back. I just can't. I can't live in a two-bedroom apartment with my kids. We can't afford private school. I can't live with my in-laws. I can't go back to an office job. I have to fix this!*

"So you and Oscar and Brice are always good?"

"Yes, because we're white. Sharu isn't. So he's bad. People with dark skin are bad."

Holy shit! My child is a racist!

"Gomer!" *Stay calm,* I thought. "Why would you say such a thing? Where did you hear this? We've never taught you that before!"

"Oscar told us. He said that he likes Spider-Man, and dark Spider-Man is bad." *Stupid superheroes!*

"Gomer, I don't know anything about Spider-Man, but I can tell you that Spider-Man has nothing to do with real people. You can't say that all dark people are bad. Look at Daddy. He isn't white. Is he bad?"

"No, because you make him okay. Oscar says that Daddy's

okay because you're not dark. You make Daddy better." *Wow, Oscar has a whole lot of theories, doesn't he? I can't wait to call his mother and have this conversation!*

"Gomer, does Oscar not like anyone who isn't white?"

"I think so. He doesn't like Nikhil, either." Nikhil was another Indian boy in the class. He was in a wheelchair. "But he won't let Nikhil play because he can't run."

So much for my empathetic and understanding child! What the hell was he learning at school?

"Gomer, this is an awful game you're playing and I forbid you to play it anymore," I told him.

"Why?"

"Because you're telling Sharu that he's bad because his skin is dark."

"You mean because he's not white."

"Gomer, stop saying that!" Suddenly I realized there was a disconnect with him. "Gomer, you do understand that you're not white, either, right?" Ever since Gomer was a baby we'd been telling him that he was half Caucasian and half Chinese. This information should not have been a surprise to Gomer, yet it appeared to be. Apparently we had not done a very good job explaining his ethnicity to him.

His face turned red, his eyes scrunched up, and he wailed, *"That's not true!"*

"Gomer, stop that. Of course it's true! What's wrong with you? You know that you're half Chinese!"

"Oscar says I'm not. Oscar says I look like I'm white, so I don't have to be a big dark monster. If I'm half Chinese, then Oscar won't play with me."

"Well, you know what? Oscar sounds like a terrible person, so I think not playing with him is a good idea anyway."

That night I called the teacher and told her about the game the boys were playing. Ms. Rebecca is one of the nicest ladies you'll ever leave your kids with, but she refuses to believe the worst about anyone.

"Sometimes this happens in preschool," she explained. "The kids are learning to sort. They sort bricks and toys, and sometimes they sort people, either by hair color or by skin color. It's just a stage they go through."

"I don't think this is a stage, Rebecca. They're excluding a child because of his skin color! That's racism."

"They're three, Jen. They don't even know what racism is."

"They do if they've been taught that at home. I want the number for Oscar's parents. I want to speak to them."

"They're on the do-not-share list. They want their number kept private."

"Are you kidding me? Of course they do, because they know their kid is a little shit!"

"I can ask the counselor to send home some book titles that might help you and Gomer work through this together."

"I don't want books from the counselor! I want to speak to Oscar's parents."

"I'm sorry, but I can't share their information with you."

"Fine. Then I at least want Oscar to be kept away from Gomer."

"There are only twelve kids in the class. How can I do that?"

"I don't know, but I want this game stopped."

"Jen, it's good for them to have imaginative play."

"Rebecca, not like this!"

"Sharu hasn't complained."

"That's because he's three! He doesn't realize what's happening. Look, I'm coming up to the school tomorrow with Gomer and I'll put an end to it if you won't."

The next day I went to class with Gomer. I quickly realized that Oscar knew *exactly* what he was doing. It wasn't a game that he played just on the playground, he played it all day long.

"No one share markers with Sharu," Oscar whispered to his classmates around the table. "He's a big dark monster."

When he saw me glare at him, he doubled down. At the circle rug he said, "Whoever sits by Sharu will be a big dark *ugly* monster."

At snack time Sharu passed out snacks, and Oscar told the group, "If you eat the big dark monster's snacks, you'll get sick and might die."

"Okay! That's it!" I announced. "Oscar, it's time for you and me to have a talk." I got down in his face and whispered, "Listen to me, Oscar. I don't know where you learned to treat people like this, but let me tell you something, it's completely unacceptable. If you continue down this path, you will grow up to be an ignorant jerk. Is that what you want? Sharu is not a bad person because he has dark skin, but *you* are a bad person, because you are stupid. He can't change his skin color, but you can change your attitude."

"I'm going to tell my mother you called me stupid!" he said.

"Oh, please do, because I would love to have your mother call me. You be sure and tell her everything I said."

When I got home that day, the Hubs met me at the door. "Do you have something you want to tell me?" he asked.

"What do you mean?" I asked innocently. *Did Oscar's mother call?*

"The school counselor called with some book suggestions for Gomer."

"Oh."

"It's weird. A lot of them are the 'I'm okay, you're okay' type."

"Okay, great."

"Jen. You were gone all day at school with Gomer, the counselor called with book selections implying our kid is going through something kind of big, and now you look guilty. What's going on?"

I couldn't keep it in any longer. I blurted out, "Gomer's a racist! We're raising a racist! It's everything you feared! He doesn't even know his ethnicity! He thinks he's white, and he thinks that everyone who is darker-colored than him is bad!"

"Oh man, is that all?" the Hubs asked.

"Is that all? Isn't that enough? Did you hear what I said? He's a racist!"

"Eh, he's a little kid. He doesn't know any better."

"He plays a game at school where they call Sharu a big dark monster and he sees nothing wrong with that. We suck as parents!"

"Jen, you're blowing it way out of proportion. Let me guess, it's that Oscar kid who started the game, right?"

"Yes. How did you know?"

"I figured. His dad gave me the once-over at drop-off a few weeks ago. I could tell he was shocked to see me with Gomer. It had never occurred to him that Gomer was biracial."

"He did? Oh shit. Now you want to move, don't you? You want to go back to New York?"

"No. I'm too spoiled by our square footage now to go back. Look, this is going to happen wherever we live. We just have to stay on top of it and do what we can to help our kids cope. But you have to let me know what's going on. I've been worried sick all day."

"You have?"

"Of course."

"I was failing at parenting."

"Well, next time, let's fail together, okay?"

"Okay."

"You freaked me out."

"I did?"

"Yeah! Look at the titles of these books: *It's Not Your Fault That You Feel Like This* and *I Know You're Sad, but It Will Be Okay.* I thought you were divorcing me!"

Oh please, Hubs. If I were divorcing you, the book title would be *Clean Out Your Closet 'Cause I'm Tired of Your Shit.*

JEEZ, LADY, I JUST WANTED A CUP OF COFFEE, NOT YOUR KIDNEY

It's hard enough for my kids to make friends, but it's even harder when I can't stand the moms. Yeah, the Hubs and I have two kids. Gomer seemed fairly easy and so we decided to roll the dice and see if we could get two easy kids. We got Adolpha. That kid was born pissed off. If anyone should be irritated, it should be Gomer. She arrived on his second birthday, forcing him to forever share *everything* from that point on—even his birthday. She cried a lot, hated to be held, and loved to hit anytime she couldn't have her own way, but Gomer was thrilled to have her. Over time she warmed up to him—but *only* him. In her eyes the rest of us are still second-class citizens compared to Gomer.

Adolpha has been anxious for a friend since she was born. She wanted to go to school at two just so she could find someone to play with. Lots of younger siblings want to go to school so they can learn to read or draw, but not Adolpha. She didn't care about reading and writing and drawing; she wanted to have playdates and sleepovers like Gomer.

As soon as she hit preschool, she started begging me to book her social calendar.

Although I'm one of the least feminine people you'll meet, I gave birth to a princess. In those days Adolpha would only wear pink or purple—preferably with a feather boa or a tiara—and she refused to play with boys. There weren't too many girls to choose from because her class was heavy on boys. I tried arranging play-dates. I asked a couple of moms if their daughters could come and play, but they had various (normal) reasons why their kids couldn't come over—dance class, gymnastics class, and so on.

"What about Evelyn?" Adolpha asked me.

"Who?" I asked.

"Evelyn. You didn't ask her."

She was right. I didn't see Evelyn's name on the list the teacher had given me. The next time I picked up Adolpha, I asked the teacher about Evelyn.

"Oh yes, they asked not to be on the contact list," the teacher told me.

"Really? That seems odd. Don't they want Evelyn to be invited to play or to birthday parties?" I asked.

"I'm not sure," the teacher replied. "Her mom is real . . . protective."

"I see," I said.

"There's Evelyn!" Adolpha yelled, tugging my hand.

I looked up and saw a woman carrying her toddler. Adolpha and I went up to them.

"Hi," I said, sticking out my hand. "I'm Jen. Adolpha's mom."

"I figured," she replied, ignoring my hand. "I've kind of got my hands full here."

Okay, she's a tough one, I thought. *Adolpha likes her kid, though, and wants a playdate. Don't screw this up.*

I continued, "So, Adolpha wanted to know if Evelyn can come over one day this week and play."

"I don't know you" was the reply I got.

I was a little taken aback. *That's harsh. Maybe she's having a bad day?* "Well, that's true. As I said before, I'm Adolpha's mom. I've been coming to this preschool for three years now. My son, Gomer, was also a student here, and we've had Ms. Rebecca the whole time. *She* knows me."

"I understand you're Adolpha's mother and maybe Ms. Rebecca knows you, but *I* don't know you. I barely know Ms. Rebecca."

I was dumbfounded. I had no idea how to reply to this.

I didn't know what else to say, so I repeated myself like an asshole: "As I said, I'm Adolpha's mother, Jen." As if that was going to make her feel better. *Ohhh, you're Jen. I didn't catch your name the first three times you said it. Thanks for continually repeating it. Now I know you!* I tried, "Adolpha would love to have Evelyn over to play. Just for an hour or so."

"I'm not comfortable having Evelyn in your house. I don't know you."

If she said "I don't know you" one more time, I was going to scream, *I don't know you, either, lady, but what the fuck is your problem?*

Now I was getting a smidge offended. It's not like I'm on a watch list of any kind!

"I don't allow Evelyn to go to anyone's home that I don't know. Terrifying things happen in other people's homes."

Now I was intrigued. "Like what?" I asked.

"Well, for instance, fires. Do you have a fire plan? I doubt it. Most homeowners don't. Do you run fire drills with your children? Do you have fire extinguishers on every floor?"

"Umm . . . we have smoke detectors," I said.

"Smoke detectors don't put out fires," she replied. "What if the girls were upstairs and a fire started and you couldn't get to them?"

"Were you in a fire?" I asked, thinking maybe that was why she was so crazy.

"Of course not. *We* have a fire plan."

I was ready to tell this lady that a "fire plan" doesn't actually prevent fires any more than my smoke detectors do, but the look on Adolpha's face made me keep going. She just wanted Evelyn to come over and play with her dolls!

"Look, it's not a big deal. I've never lived in a house that has caught fire, we don't keep weapons in our house, I can follow any kind of dietary restrictions you might have, and we can put Barbie away if you think she's not a positive body image role model for girls. My son, Gomer, is having a friend over on Friday, and Adolpha wants to have Evelyn come, too. She would like a friend, and she would like Evelyn to be that friend."

"Your son and another boy will be there, too?" she asked.

"Yes," I said, getting my hopes up. Would that make a difference?

"I'm very uncomfortable letting Evelyn be alone around older boys."

Older boys? "Gomer's six."

"Plus, now that's four children you would need to get out in the event of a fire."

Motherf—

"Okay. How about this? How about you and Evelyn come over? I'll make some coffee and I'll buy some muffins and we can chat and you can *get to know* me while Adolpha and Evelyn play where we can see them in a match-free environment while the boys play up in Gomer's room and never come near the girls," I offered helpfully.

"I'm not comfortable with that, either," she said. "That means both Evelyn and I would be in a stranger's home."

Oh, for fuck's sake, lady! You're killing me!

I was at my wits' end. I just wanted a friend for Adolpha. This was getting ridiculous. What did this woman want from me?

"All right, then you tell me what you *are* comfortable with. Adolpha would like to play with Evelyn outside school. How do you usually make that happen?"

This was my last attempt. If this didn't work, I was going to tell the woman to go fuck herself.

"We don't. Evelyn only plays with people I know. And *I don't know you.*"

I looked at Adolpha, who was ready to cry, and so was I. What a fucking bitch. Who treats people like this? Somehow I missed the news bulletin about the suburban moms who lure other suburban moms into their homes, dope them with tainted coffee, and then steal their internal organs to sell on the black market.

What was this woman's problem? We are all wary of strangers and concerned about where our kids are going and whom they will be with, but this woman was taking it entirely too far. If she didn't want her kid to go to a stranger's house, then get to know me at least so I'm not a stranger anymore. At least offer to meet me at a fast-food playland and risk a staph infection and have a cup of coffee!

It wasn't just Adolpha looking for a friend. I was hoping to find another mom or two that I could relate to. I'd love to have a friend or two to hang out with while our girls trash my house. Obviously this woman was not going to make the cut and receive the other half of my BFF necklace.

I didn't know what her problem was. Maybe she truly was afraid of strangers. If she was that afraid, then she needed professional help. Also, she needed to figure out a nicer, kinder way to explain her phobias, because I couldn't help but take it personally. She didn't want to go to *my* crappy tinderbox of a house and be exposed to my predatory son and his friend. And worst of all, she didn't want her daughter to be friends with *my* daughter.

"You know what?" I said to her. "You're right, you don't know me, and let's keep it that way, because I'm exhausted by you. I don't want to know you and hear about your fire safety drills and whatever else keeps you up at night. But the one who is really missing out is Evelyn. Adolpha is the kind of friend everyone wishes for. She is fiercely loyal, funny, and a little bit zany. Your kid would be lucky to have Adolpha in her life, but she missed that chance because her mother is a lunatic."

I threw my nose in the air, grabbed Adolpha's hand, and stormed off toward my car praying to God that I didn't stumble in a pothole and embarrass myself any more than I already had. "Don't worry, Adolpha," I whispered. "*I* will be your best friend."

"But you're so old," she whined.

"Yeah, but I have money. I take my best friends shopping. Let's go and buy something great."

"Like a puppy?" she asked hopefully.

"Don't push it, kid, or I'll make Gomer my best friend."

HELLO MOTHER, HELLO FATHER, SIGNING UP FOR CAMP SUCKS

I never send my kids to camp in the summer. Not because I don't have the money, but because I don't have the organizational skills to do it.

Do you know how early in the year you have to register for summer camps? It is unbelievable. I just get the Christmas decorations packed away when my inbox starts filling up with reminders of fast-approaching deadlines for summer camp. And it's not like choosing a camp is an easy decision. There are dozens to choose from. My kids could go to a different camp every day if I could afford it.

Here are just some of the many camps we have to choose from:

Soccer
Baseball
Basketball
Football
Golf
Tennis

Racquetball

Swimming

Cheerleading

Ice skating

Dance (ballet, jazz, tap, interpretive, water ballet,
    competitive jazz aerobics)

Swimming (competitive and synchronized)

Diving

Gymnastics

Tae kwon do

Karate

Fencing

Hockey

Kindermusik

Art classes (painting, sculpture, drawing, pottery, etc.)

Computer classes (animation, robotics, programming, etc.)

Instrument lessons (violin and piano seem to be the
    dominant ones right now)

Math Monkey

Kumon

Foreign languages (Spanish, French, Chinese)

Scouts

Daisies

Cooking

And I know I'm missing a bunch.

The possibilities are endless. Adolpha could take an advanced
hair-braiding course at the community center while Gomer
learns Chinese calligraphy. But only if I get off my ass and figure
out what we're going to be doing in six months.

Six months? That's a long time away. I barely know what I'm

doing next week; I can't possibly plan for six months from now. What if an all-expenses-paid trip is offered to us and Gomer's already enrolled in pizza-making camp? Plus, my children's interests are fickle. How can I be sure Adolpha will still be interested in attending Robotics for Grrrls in six months?

Also, we all know that even though there are thousands of camps offered every summer, there are only a handful that are really sought after. I don't know who decides each year what the hot new camps will be, but someone does and word spreads fast to everyone except me. I'm always the last to know, and then I'm scrambling to try to get my kids in cool camps, too. If I want to get Adolpha into dressage camp, then not only do I have to plan our calendar six months out, but I also have to get up at the ass crack of dawn to get online and make sure I get one of the few coveted spots or else she's going to end up in mime camp—and try explaining mime camp to a five-year-old. Good luck!

When Adolpha was about three I let the pressure get to me. I fell for the hype and enrolled her in dance camp, which was supposed to be *the* camp that year. It was my first experience with "girl moms," and I blame them. Totally. In case you don't know what a girl mom is, I'll explain. A girl mom is more than just a mom with a daughter. A girl mom is someone who takes her girls to a whole new level of girliness. She usually dresses her newborn daughter in tutus and little socks that look like high-heeled shoes and quickly moves her into faux fur. I am not a girl mom, but by the time Adolpha was three it was readily apparent to anyone watching that Adolpha *wished* I was a girl mom. I was raising the girliest girl on the block. I had a toddler on my hands who literally ripped clothing off her body Hulk-style if it wasn't "pink enough," wailed for sparkly high heels, and rocked tiaras and wild tights most days. If Adolpha didn't look exactly like the

Hubs, I would have wondered if perhaps the hospital had accidentally switched babies and I was raising some random girl mom's baby while she struggled to raise a girl who wanted to wear overalls and sensible shoes.

I encountered these girl moms at a playdate at a neighbor's house. We'd been invited for a "teddy bear tea party" playdate. (Girl moms like to give everything a theme, even playdates. It helps the hostess plan snacks and lets attendees know what the expected attire is.) The little girls were off giggling in the playroom eating their custom-made teddy bear cupcakes when Rose, one of the moms, complained, "Who's ready for tomorrow?"

A chorus of groans resounded around the room. I was flummoxed.

"Oh, it's going to be awful," sighed Melody, the hostess.

"Last year I barely got Kenadi enrolled," said Lori, the woman next to me. "I was second to last. I couldn't believe it."

I tried to figure out what they were talking about. What had I missed? School enrollment? No, it was January, so that was still a ways off.

When Melody saw my confused expression, she said, "Oh, Jen! I forgot you were here! You probably have no idea what we're talking about. We all attend dance together. We're planning on enrolling in Ms. Tiffani-Anne's School of Dance Super-Duper Summer Blowout Dance Camp for Little Hoofers."

Ohhhh yeah. I forgot: a girl mom usually has a history of dance in her past and is anxious to get her little darling on the boards as soon as possible.

"Is Adolpha a dancer?" asked Lori.

"No. She's three," I replied. No three-year-old should ever

classify herself as anything—she's barely human at that point—but especially not a dancer.

Everyone chuckled, but I could tell from their side glances at one another that they were not amused.

"Jen, wouldn't you *like* for Adolpha to be a dancer?" Melody asked me.

"God, no! Why would I want that?" I exclaimed before I could filter myself.

"Excuse me?"

"Well," I said, trying to fix my blunder, "dancers are kind of a mess. I read a book about ballerinas when I was ten years old and every single one of them was a binger and a purger and cheated at school so she could keep dancing. It made me realize that I never wanted my daughters to be ballerinas—or anorexic. I've seen that dance show on TLC or whatever with the fat woman who yells at the little girls. Those kids are like eight years old and they look like harlots when they dance. I have no desire to raise my daughter for a life on the pole. If it's not ballet or pole dancing, what other kind of dancing is there? I guess maybe she could clog, but the hair on those girls looks like an insane amount of work, and she's half Chinese and her other half isn't Irish."

"Jen, do you know how I know everyone here today—except for you, of course?" Melody asked.

"No."

"We were all Jazzy Jaguars together in college."

I choked on my tea biscuit. "What the fuck is a Jazzy Jaguar?"

"Only the greatest college-level dance team in the southeastern United States," said Melody.

"Our senior year we won the Southeastern United States Regional Dance Competition—Small to Mid-Sized College Division."

"The awards were great, but we got so much more than that out of dancing," said Lori.

"Poise and athleticism," mumbled Rose as she stuffed another muffin in her mouth and brushed the crumbs off her no longer poised and athletic belly.

"Mental toughness," said Melody, moving Rose's plate out of her reach and giving her hand a pat.

"Friendship," said Lori, smiling at Melody and Rose.

That's what did it. That smile. Sure, these women annoyed the hell out of me and intimidated the crap out of me. I could never invite them into my cluttered home for a non-themed playdate where I'd serve boxed cookies and non-organic juice boxes. I could never go with them to get drinks at the newest, coolest, hippest bar in town—mostly because I had nothing to wear to such a place. I was a lost cause, and some days I am perfectly okay with that. But that day I worried about my daughter. I'd chosen a path of not giving a damn for myself, but was it fair to force that on Adolpha? She obviously wanted more. She wanted poise and athleticism and mental toughness and ridiculous fluffy costumes. But most of all, she wanted friends. I could hear her playing in the next room and I knew she was having fun. She wanted to belong to a group and to find girls she could grow up with. I knew that meant I'd have to get along with the mothers, but I was willing to do that for Adolpha, because that's what mothers do.

"I want in," I said.

"What?" asked Melody.

"How do I sign up? I want Adolpha to be a dancer."

"I thought it wasn't something you wanted for her," said Rose.

"Dancing was never anything I've been interested in, but I think Adolpha would love it. I don't want her in some half-assed program. If we're going to do this, I want to be in the best. Is Ms. Tiffani-Anne the best?"

"Of course she is!" said Melody.

"You have to be serious if you're going to join," said Lori. "Ms. Tiffani-Anne is not for the casual dancer. She only takes the best."

"There's a tryout?" I gasped. Adolpha could barely walk in a straight line—how would she make it through a tryout?

"No, nothing like that," said Melody. "She just expects the girls to work hard."

"No problem. We can do that," I said.

"Well, then it sounds like you'll be joining us tomorrow morning," said Lori.

"Right. What do I have to do?"

"We get on line at four A.M.," said Melody.

"Online? What's the web address?" I asked, dreading getting up so early to log on to my computer.

"No, you misunderstood. On line," said Rose. "Literally. We line up outside the studio at four A.M. Doors open at seven. Ms. Tiffani-Anne takes the first two hundred who make the cut."

"Who make the cut? So there *is* a tryout," I said.

"There's an interview process," said Melody. "If you line up with us, you'll be fine."

That's how I found myself standing out in the freezing cold at four the next morning. When I arrived, Melody, Rose, and Lori were several people ahead of me. I didn't even try to join them in line; I could tell that the women behind us would shiv me if I tried.

I stood there for the next hour trying to will my body not to go into hypothermic shock.

"Excuse me?" asked the woman in front of me, obviously quite offended.

"Huh?" I said.

"Did you just say, 'What the fuck am I doing here?'"

"Did I?" I was definitely thinking it. I must have said it out loud.

"You certainly did," her friend replied.

"You know, there are hundreds of women lined up behind you who would kill for your spot right now, and you've got that kind of attitude?"

"Well, I'm freezing. This is so stupid. I can't believe I'm here," I whined. "I've been lined up in the cold for an hour to get a three-year-old into a dance camp. What is wrong with me?"

"If you're not committed, you're never going to make it anyway," said the woman behind me. "Ms. Tiffani-Anne only wants committed children and mommies. Sounds like you're not committed."

"I *should* be committed! I'm fucking crazy. She's three. Do you know what I did in the summertime when I was three? I swam with floaties and rode my Big Wheel. That's it. Nope, I'm done. Good luck, ladies." And with that I stepped out of line and the group surged to fill my hole.

"Jen!" called Melody. "There are only a couple more hours left. I thought you wanted this for Adolpha."

"Where's her mental toughness?" whispered Rose.

"She has none. She never danced," Lori whispered back.

I stepped away and looked at the line snaking through the

parking lot. I wanted to scream: *Why the fuck are we doing this? Are we afraid they're going to fall behind in the world of dance and soccer and pizza making and miming?* We talk a lot about camps broadening their minds and teaching them things like responsibility and leadership skills, but really I think most moms are using those four hours a day to just be alone. I think we're afraid of the idea of spending all day with our kids.

I realize parenting is hard and boring at times and a four-hour break would be super, but this is the job we signed up for. Some days it sucks, but most days it's great. I like my days when my kids are in school, but I also like my summers with them. I like going to the pool and bowling and traveling with them. I also like sending them to their rooms for an hour to read—I've got to get my reading time in, too!

So while I might not have the mental tenacity to stand in line for three hours in January, I do have the mental tenacity to get through a summer with my kids.

OOH, SORRY TO HEAR YOU GOT AGNES IN YOUR CLASS, BUT I HEAR HER MOTHER IS LOVELY

I'll admit that when Gomer started kindergarten he was a bit sheltered. Okay, he was *a lot* sheltered. He still let me pick out his clothes every day, I was known as "Mommy," he slept with a blankie that he called "munga-munga" (don't ask—I have no idea where that name came from), and his best friend was his baby sister.

(Actually, now that I reread that paragraph, not much has changed now that Gomer is eight. I still pick out his clothes, mostly because he's too lazy to decide what to wear and/or he would choose shorts every single day regardless of the weather, munga-munga is somewhere in his bed and I'm pretty certain he snuggles with it when no one is watching, and his sister is still his best friend. The part that has changed the most is the fact that I'm no longer "Mommy." I'd settle for "Mom," but instead, I'm usually "dude." WTF?)

He'd been out in the real world for a couple of years at preschool, but preschool, aside from a few potentially racist games, was a sheltering environment, where he was adored, loved, and coddled like a prized calf. That kid was so soft, he would cry out of sympathy if his sister got into trouble.

The Hubs and I knew kindergarten would be a bit of an adjustment for him. We knew that suddenly he would be forced to share space with twenty-plus kids and (gasp) only one teacher. We knew there would be some tough days for him. We just never thought he'd get the shit beaten out of him.

The first week of school, I was putting Gomer to bed and I asked about his day. "It was awful, Mommy," he sobbed. "I got attacked on the playground!"

"What?" I asked, my mind racing. *Who attacked my precious baby? I'll kill that kid!* "Who attacked you, Gomer?"

"Agnes," he whimpered.

Agnes! Of course! Oh, I knew who Agnes was. I'd been warned about her on the first day of school.

I had just dropped off Gomer in his new classroom when I stopped to say hello to my friend Sandy in the hallway. As I was catching up Sandy on my family's scintillating summer vacation in Branson (don't judge—my kids think Branson is just as good as Disney), we saw Agnes dart out of the classroom to grab a drink from the water fountain.

"Hey, Agnes," the teacher called. "Please come back in here. We don't leave the room without permission, please."

"I'm sorry. I was thirsty!" Agnes said, never moving from her position by the water fountain.

The teacher ducked back into the classroom and Agnes stayed put, kicking the wall. Then she reached up and ripped the picture from the *Very Hungry Caterpillar* bulletin board. The caterpillar's red head drifted to the floor, where Agnes ground it into the carpet with her tennis shoe.

What the hell, kid? I wondered. *You'd better get your butt back in the classroom before you get in big trouble.*

"Agnes?" The teacher popped her head out again.

Agnes instantly straightened up and smiled while covering the obliterated caterpillar head with her shoe. "Yes, ma'am?"

"Are you coming, dear?"

I thought, *What's with all the questions? Just tell her to move it.*

"In a minute," she said. *In a minute? Are you allowed to say that to a teacher now?* Agnes turned her attention back to the bulletin board. She started digging a hole in the cork.

"Oh, it's a good thing I'm not a teacher," I mumbled to Sandy. "Can you still spank kids at school?"

Sandy giggled, and the teacher frowned at her. "Excuse me," Sandy said, looking at her feet.

"I have to go to the bathroom," said Agnes.

"Okay, but hurry up," the teacher said. She went back in the room.

Sandy and I continued our conversation until we heard a scream from the girls' room. A girl ran out clutching her bloody mouth.

"What happened?" Sandy asked.

The teacher ran out of the classroom. "What is going on out here?" she demanded as Agnes exited the bathroom and took a real interest in washing her hands in the community sink between both bathrooms. I kept an eye on Agnes as she soaped up.

"She pushed me into the wall and my tooth fell out," the girl wailed, pointing at Agnes, who continued to scrub up like she was going into surgery.

"Who, me?" Agnes asked innocently. "I didn't push you. The floor was slippery. I actually slipped earlier. I was going to tell you, but you fell before I could. Good news is, the tooth fairy will come tonight."

The injured girl actually smiled. *Whoa, this kid is good.*

"I will let the janitor know there is a slick spot in there. Sally, you may go see the nurse. Agnes, are you coming?"

"Yes, ma'am. I was just trying to fix this bulletin board."

"Oh, you're such a sweet girl," the teacher said, giving Sandy and me a smile that said, *Isn't she precious?*

Sandy coughed into her hand, and it sounded a lot like she said, "Devil," but I can't be certain.

The teacher said to Agnes, "I worked for hours on that bulletin board. It's always so sad when they get wrecked. I was hoping it would at least last the week. Oh well, come in now, dear. I'll stay after school today and fix it." She went back in the classroom.

"*You* wrecked it," I said to Agnes as she sauntered past me.

I looked helplessly at Sandy. She coughed again. "Jerk." This time I heard her clearly.

"No. It was already ripped when I found it. I just brushed into it and then it ripped some more. It was an accident," Agnes said, looking at me with giant doe eyes. "Especially when this part fell off." She held up two mangled green construction paper pears.

"Come along, Agnes," the teacher called.

"Coming, ma'am. This strange lady was talking to me and I was telling her that I'm not allowed to talk to strangers," Agnes said as she ran into the classroom, stuffing construction paper down her skort.

The teacher looked at us sternly. "Ladies, the bell has rung. It might be better to take your conversation to the parking lot so you don't disturb the students."

I just got scolded by a teacher! *Are you joking? That kid set me up.*

"I'm not a stranger," I said. "I'm Gomer's mother. They're

classmates. Agnes is treating me like I tried to lure her into my van with candy or a puppy!"

"We take stranger danger very seriously in this school. If she was uncomfortable with your attention, she has every right to say so. And because you are a classmate's mother, you should know better than to make her afraid," the teacher replied coldly.

"But she ruined your bulletin board, and I'm pretty sure she pushed that kid," I tried.

"Excuse me?" the teacher said. "Children fall all the time at school. Bulletin boards get ruined. These are accidents. Agnes is a child. She is not malicious. *She* did nothing wrong. Now, *you* ladies . . . well, I believe the principal sent out an email asking all of the parents to leave the building by the last bell so that we can start our day of learning."

"That kid is a mess," Sandy muttered as we walked toward the lobby of the school.

"Do you know her?" I asked.

"Yeah. Don't you?" she asked.

"No. I've never seen her before. I've met her mother at different things, but I haven't had the pleasure of seeing her in action. She's a bit of a handful, isn't she?"

"Ha! She's worse than that. Is that Gomer's classroom?"

"Yes."

"Ooh, sorry to hear that. She's a real pain in the ass, but her mother is delightful—go figure."

"How do you know her?"

"I told you about her. She's the biter," Sandy said.

Last year Agnes was in preschool with Sandy's daughter, Zara, and she'd had quite a few run-ins with her. She stole her snack for several weeks, and then when Zara finally told on her, she started kicking her on the playground. Sandy set up an appointment to meet with the school director and the teacher to discuss the problem. They mentioned then that they'd had several complaints about Agnes for kicking, hitting, and pinching but that that no one on staff had ever seen her do anything like that. The teacher went on and on about what a wonderful woman her mother was and how she couldn't possibly be as bad as everyone claimed. She even suggested that maybe, just maybe, the other kids in the class were jealous of Agnes and were making up stories about her. They basically called Zara a liar. Sandy was livid, but there wasn't much she could do. She told Zara to stay away from her, but then one day during rest period Agnes bit her. She bit her so hard she bled. Zara woke up and saw it was Agnes clamped down on her arm like a rabid dog, but by the time the staff got there, Agnes was back in her bed pretending to be asleep. Sandy could never prove it was Agnes, but she pulled Zara out of school after that.

The biter. Her?

I thought about Agnes. She was a tiny little thing, barely bigger than my preschooler. But her reputation was *huge*. I had always assumed she was a hulking brute with a skull-and-bones tattoo on her biceps and the rasp of a smoker. This little girl had pigtails, a button nose, and an adorable lisp that was exaggerated by her two missing front teeth.

Sandy wasn't the only one who'd had problems with Agnes. Although I'd never seen the little terror in person, I'd heard so many stories about kids with broken arms, stitches, or black eyes. There was never enough proof to flat-out blame Agnes, but she was always conveniently close by when a child "accidentally" fell out of a tree house and broke an arm or when her next-door neighbor's pit bull "escaped" from his enclosure to terrorize the block.

The rumor around the carpool line was the principal didn't know which class to put her in, because so many parents were upset with Agnes and they demanded that she not be in their child's class. I didn't even know you could do such a thing— those parents with older kids always know the loopholes. Now my kid was stuck with her!

It was awkward, though, because everyone loves Agnes's mom. With her witty sense of humor and friendly personality, she's a favorite at her neighborhood Moms' Night Out or her exclusive invitation-only book club. Everyone—myself included— wanted to be her friend.

"Well, maybe she's not so bad," I said hopefully, trying not to think about Sally's prematurely lost tooth and my name lingering on the wait list for Agnes's mother's book club.

"She—and her mother—have everyone snowed. She's the first to volunteer at any classroom party to bring a healthy snack that the kids will actually eat. She's always got great ideas for a game or a craft to keep them occupied during the party. She's happy to volunteer whenever you need her. Librarian needs help reshelving books? She's on it. Reading specialist needs someone to listen to the kids read out loud? No problem. Janitor needs help cleaning the urinals? It's not something she's used to doing, but she's happy to help! And don't forget: that kid accused you of stranger danger. That's a big deal around here."

Oh yeah. What *was* that all about? What the hell, Agnes? That shit is serious, kid. This was my first year in the school; can you imagine what would happen to me if *that* story got started? With a stranger danger strike against me, I'd never get to be a room mom.

"She's a little shit. She pushes their buttons. Watch out for her," Sandy advised me. "The upside, though, is if Agnes beats up your kid, you get a nice gift. I love my planter."

Soon after Zara started at her new school, Sandy told me, a planter and a gift basket arrived on Sandy's porch. They were from Agnes's mom. The basket was full of all kinds of cool shit that Sandy would never buy herself and a gift card for a massage. It's kind of Agnes's mom's MO. She never admits her guilt, but the gift basket is a kind of apology for when Agnes hurts your kid. Everyone knows it. Just about every house on Sandy's block has a beautiful planter on the porch. One neighbor even has a new cherry tree, because Agnes chopped hers down on President's Day after she studied George Washington. "She has such a love of American history!" was what her mother said as she wrote the check for the tree.

From that day forward I started to keep an eye on Agnes, just like Sandy had suggested.

I didn't see much out of the ordinary. She pulled a lot of Eddie Haskell shit when I worked in the classroom: "You look very nice today, ma'am." "Thank you for volunteering in our classroom today." "I'm so happy you're here today!"

I wanted to say, *Cut the crap, kid. I'm a tired thirty-seven-year-old woman in mom jeans. Even my husband doesn't think I look nice today.*

Although Agnes was smarmy and seemed poised to have an excellent career in sales and/or politics, I had never witnessed her being violent, so it did surprise me when Gomer said Agnes had "attacked" him. Maybe Gomer felt attacked by Agnes's bullshit. I know I did.

"What did Agnes do to you?" I asked Gomer.

"I told you. She attacked me," Gomer sniffled.

"But *how* did she attack you? Did she bite you?" I asked, thinking of Zara.

"She punches me at recess. She does it when the teachers aren't looking."

"Well, did you tell your teacher?"

"No! I can't! Agnes says, 'Snitches get stitches.' That means if you tattle you get hit harder."

WTF, where did that come from? Agnes didn't get that from Nickelodeon. "Yes, I know what that means."

"Well, I didn't. I had to ask Agnes, and she punched me again while she told me. Just like she does every day!"

Every day, and I was just now hearing about this?

Now, at this point you might think I'm a terrible mother, because I'm not freaking out and calling the school and Agnes's mother and filing a restraining order against the little asshole. But you must understand: Gomer has an overactive imagination. Oh, screw it, let's be honest—Gomer can be a big fat liar.

You must proceed with extreme caution when Gomer tells you a story about school, because you're never quite sure if it's true or not. I've been burned a few times now by flying off the handle and assuming that my precious baby was telling me the God's honest truth, only to find out he'd pieced together several episodes of *Wonder Pets* and *The Backyardigans* to create his epic tale of woe. (This should probably be a lesson for me to pay more attention to what he's watching on TV, but then what's the point of plopping him in front of the TV to use it as a babysitter if I have to sit there, too? Duh.)

Honestly, if Sandy hadn't told me to keep an eye on Agnes, I probably would have called Gomer a liar and said goodnight. But I'd seen the stitches on that snitch Zara.

"Okay, Gomer. Don't worry. Daddy and I will take care of it."

I tucked him in and then went downstairs to figure out what to do.

I was hesitant to contact Agnes's mother, because it could easily spiral out of control and I can only imagine how that conversation might go:

Jen: Hi, this is Jen, Gomer's mom. Listen, I was talking to Gomer tonight and he mentioned that Agnes has been punching him several times a day.

Agnes's mom: Oh, Jen, I'm actually glad you called.

Jen: You are? Great. I'd love to get this worked out between the two of us so they could be friends. [To myself I'm saying, *I am a parenting genius! In a year, when we're all best friends, we're going to laugh about this story.*]

Agnes's mom: Yes, I'm glad you called, because I've been hesitant to contact you. Apparently Gomer has taught Agnes the word "fuck" and now we can't stop her from using it all the time.

Jen: Wait. What? I'm shocked. Gomer doesn't even know that word.

Agnes's mom: Well, of course he does. He taught it to Agnes.

Jen: No, I'm sure he didn't.

Agnes's mom: Look, I've read your blog, and I know you use that word *allll* the time. [*Okay,* I think, *we are not going to laugh about this story.*]

Jen: Yeah, but—

Agnes's mom: I realize you think it's funny for a six-year-old to say "fuck," but I really don't.

Jen: Hold on. I don't think that's funny. Honestly, I don't use that kind of language in front of my kids. I really don't.

Agnes's mom: Look, I try not to judge other people's parenting, but I would have to say you are really terrible at it. You use that word all the time, and you probably use it when you're talking to Gomer.

Jen: I do not!

Agnes's mom: Like I said, I have no idea. I really don't care. It's none of my business what goes on in your house. All I know is that Gomer taught it to Agnes, along with all of its proper uses. She got kicked out of Sunday school last week for telling her teacher to "fuck off." That is unacceptable behavior in *this* house.

Jen: Of course it is. But are you sure it was Gomer? It just doesn't sound like him.

Agnes's mom: Oh, but Agnes strikes you as a child who punches people? I've never had a complaint about Agnes's behavior. Until she learned the *f*-word from *your* son.

Jen: My son doesn't know that word! And yes, Agnes *does* strike me as the sort of child who punches people. My husband went to the school during recess and he saw Agnes punch Gomer.

Agnes's mom: Your husband—a grown man—took off time from work to go to the school in the middle of the day to spy on children? What sort of creeper does that?

Jen: He's not a creeper!

Agnes's mom: Did he have permission to be on school property?

Jen: He drove over and watched from his car. And he saw—

Agnes's mom: Like some deranged Peeping Tom!

Jen: He saw your juvenile delinquent punch Gomer!

Agnes's mom: You know, I wasn't even going to call you—

but you've got a lot of nerve, lady, calling me up to complain about *my* daughter when your *husband* is up at the school intimidating and scaring a little girl.

Jen: My husband didn't go near your daughter. He just watched to see if Gomer was telling the truth.

Agnes's mom: *Oh!* So you thought maybe Gomer had made up the whole story about Agnes? That's interesting. Let's see if I can get this straight: you think your child *is* a liar, but he *doesn't* know the *f*-word? You live in a bubble!

Jen: This is getting ridiculous. I called you because Agnes has been punching Gomer and we'd like it to stop or else I'm going to speak with the principal.

Agnes's mom: Well, I'm going to have to speak to the principal about Gomer's language and your husband's disgusting behavior! That is stranger danger! We take that very seriously at our school!

Jen: My son doesn't know that word and my husband did nothing wrong! It's your kid who is the problem here.

Agnes's mom: My kid? My daughter has been banned from her Sunday school and now her *eternal soul* is in jeopardy thanks to your kid! What do you have to say for yourself?

Jen: Fuck you!

See why I needed more information? Calling up another mother without the whole story is like walking into a minefield.

The Hubs and I decided that he'd go up to the school (with full permission from the principal), observe the kids during their recess, and report back so we could make a plan. He saw that Gomer was telling the truth and that it wasn't just Gomer getting the shit kicked out of him. Agnes hid out behind the play structure where the teachers couldn't see her and whenever an unsuspecting student would drift into her area, Agnes would tackle the child and pummel them.

We contacted the teacher and told her about what the Hubs had witnessed. We asked her to keep an eye on the kids and let us know what she saw. Her reply to my initial email was, "I'm so surprised to hear that Gomer and Agnes aren't getting along! Agnes just adores Gomer and spends as much time as she can with him. Sure, she's a bit handsy with her friends, but she's got a lot of energy bottled up in that little body and it's hard at this age to keep your excitement contained. I'll speak with both of them and make sure they understand how we treat our friends. By the way, have you met Agnes's mother? She's a lovely woman and does so much for our school! She's coming in today to redo my bulletin board—she'd heard it had been vandalized and she offered to fix it. I'll just mention this email to her and I'm sure we can get the situation with Gomer and Agnes sorted out right away."

Within a week I received a gift. I came home from running errands and I found a large package on my front porch. It was a cool, upcycled metal bucket that you can only get at some trendy store I would never set foot in, filled with whimsical gifts for the family: giant marbles and fake mustaches for the kids, a Riding Mower–scented Yankee Candle for the Hubs, and tons of booze and cocktail napkins covered in pictures of perky 1950s house-wives with snarky thought bubbles over their heads for me: *I just made a batch of shut the fucupcakes!*

There was a note attached:

Dear Jen,

    I don't think we've actually met yet—we have several mutual friends, and I think I was introduced to you at the

Joneses' back-to-school blowout a few weeks ago. I've heard so much about Gomer that I feel like I know you already! Agnes just adores Gomer and they have the best time together. You might have heard through the grapevine that whenever I see something that reminds me of Agnes's friends I can't help but buy it for them! It's such a bad habit, but I can't stop myself!

I thought Adolpha would like the marbles and Gomer would look fabulous in a mustache. I don't know your husband's tastes, but if he's anything like mine, he'll love this manly scented candle. I've been following your blog for some time and it's so neat to have a "celebrity" (can I call you a celebrity, or does that embarrass you?) so close by. I saw these napkins and I just thought, "Those are perfect for Jen!"

I hope you like your gifts and I can't wait to get a chance to spend some time with you. I'm working on fast-tracking your membership into the book club. I know it can take forever to get off the wait list, but I'll see if I can't get the girls to make an exception for you!

Maybe Gomer can come for a playdate soon? I know Agnes would love that!

Best, Agnes's mom

Oh wow, I thought. *She really is thoughtful! Those napkins are perfect for me and she called me a "celebrity." No one's ever called me a celebrity before. Maybe Agnes isn't that bad. Her mom has terrific taste, after all. She bought adorable gifts and she thinks I'm a celebrity! Plus she's working on my book club membership. I've been on that damn list for a year!*

Later that day, Gomer came home with a torn shirt and a

bruised arm. "Look what Agnes did!" he cried as soon as he walked in the door.

Fuck, I thought as I laid down the February book club selection (I figured I'd start reading it just in case I made it through the background check before the meeting next week). I looked at Gomer's tearstained face and caught a whiff of the Riding Mower candle that was burning on the counter. It smelled heavenly. *He's had that shirt for a couple of years,* I thought, *so it probably didn't take* that *much force to rip it.* The ice in my midday cocktail shifted (yes, I was having a midday cocktail; I like a cocktail when I read, so sue me). I picked up my glass and a mischievous housewife grinned at me from the napkin ("It's wine-thirty somewhere!"). *Kids fall down. Shirts get ripped. It's not* that *big a deal, right?* I thought.

"Mommy!" Gomer cried. "She kicked me in my pee-pee!"

Damn that Agnes—and her mother!

I blew out the Riding Mower–scented candle, shoved my new napkins in a drawer, and picked up the phone.

I'd like to say the situation was resolved quickly, but it wasn't.

Over the course of the school year I received two more lovely gift baskets and a beautiful planter for my porch. I was fast-tracked into the book club, and Agnes's mother picked my book for our December selection.

The following year I requested Agnes not be in the same classroom as Gomer, but I am loving book club with Agnes's mother, because she really is wonderful.

THOU SHALT NOT COVET THY NEIGHBOR'S SWEET-ASS RIDE

I have a confession to make. No, this isn't the part where I reveal that I'm a closet crafter who has a craft room in my basement where I hoard countless dollars' worth of rubber stamps, paint, tulle, ribbon, and glue guns (yes, glue guns, plural, because every good crafter worth her glitter knows you need more than one size). Even though that's all true, I'd rather talk about my even more embarrassing confession: I want a minivan. *Baaad.*

It's not like I *need* a minivan. I have only two children and no pets that I need to haul around town. I just really *want* one. In black, preferably, because black is more badass, and why wouldn't I want to drive a badass minivan?

I know, I know. Most people think that nothing says "defeat" quite like a minivan. I get it. It isn't a sexy car. It looks a little soft and frumpy. The minivan is the yoga pants of vehicles. But you know what? I *love* my yoga pants. And my yoga pants would look *good* behind the wheel of a new mobile command center (or MCC, as we minivan lovers prefer to call it).

The people who turn up their noses at minivans typically opt for the SUV. To them the SUV still has enough room to haul strollers, diaper bags, soccer cleats, ballet costumes, school bags, an extra kid for a playdate, and the family dog, all while still looking hip and young and cool. I know, because I used to be one of those people. For many years I prided myself on the fact that if I was caught in a freak blizzard I could throw my vehicle into four-wheel drive and safely guide my family to Target for milk and toilet paper. Or I could hook up a boat or a camper (or anything else that required hauling) to my gleaming trailer hitch and hit the open road for an impromptu getaway. I just ignored the fact that I never needed to use my all-wheel drive because I live in Kansas and not the Alps, I prefer four-star hotels to campers, and a trailer hitch is just an invitation for some asshole friend to ask you to help him move a sofa. (Wait—Hubs just told me I never had four-wheel drive. My SUVs weren't *that* tough.)

If the minivan is the yoga pants of the vehicle world, then the SUV is the cargo pants, and while I like my cargo pants just fine, let's face it: yoga pants are way more comfortable and make my ass look better. I think a minivan could do that for me, too.

My minivan coveting started a few years ago. As my kids (and I) got older, the SUV was becoming kind of a hassle. Pulling open doors is strenuous. Lifting that heavy tailgate is tough. Not having enough seats for my kids and their friends is embarrassing. I hated that I always had to say, "I can't take anyone, because my car can only hold two booster seats." If I had my sweet swagger wagon, I would have a whole row of extra seats available!

I watched with envy as the mothers around me would hit a button and their slidey doors (what else would you call them?) would open and close. I wanted that! I wanted to push a button and see my kids jump out of my van like daredevil parachuters at an air show. I would barely have to slow my roll in the pickup line at school—just pop the button and watch the kids eject themselves. Plus those slidey doors would come in handy, because my children are the sort who throw open their doors and ram them into the cars parked next to us. The people who park next to me would appreciate it if I drove a minivan. It's almost like I'd be helping mankind.

If I had a minivan, I wouldn't stop with just the automatic doors. I couldn't possibly stop there. My dream is to drive a bad-ass minivan, not just an ordinary minivan, so I'd also need the DVD player with the wireless headphones (please God, with headphones, because I can't listen to *Phineas and Ferb* while I'm driving—I'll drive off a cliff), the plugs for everyone's electronics (because no one plays I Spy on road trips anymore), Bluetooth (hands-free calling is safer—and another reason for the headphones, because "fuck you" comes up in my phone conversations more than you'd think), a sunroof (because Adolpha and I like to have the sun on our heads while we roll down the boulevard singing our hearts out), the power tailgate (no sense getting my hands dirty when that's an option), and leather seats and the leather-wrapped steering wheel (just 'cause I like "leathah"). In some ways my minivan would be nicer than my home, but I don't think that's too much to ask when you consider how much time I have to spend in my vehicle. I've never added up the weekly hours spent shuttling people around, because that number would probably make me hurt someone, but let's just say it's a lot. However, the feeling I would get from sipping a hot beverage (from one of the insane number of cupholders) and sitting on my soft and toasty-warm heated seat while waiting for soccer practice to end would be priceless.

The reason I don't currently have a minivan is because the Hubs has deemed it an impractical car for our family (and I think he thinks he'd look like a wuss driving it). I know he's right—he would look pretty wussy driving it—but who cares? It's no different from sitting outside a dressing room and holding my purse or buying feminine hygiene products by himself at the grocery store. He's already done both of these, so what is he holding out for? Of course a minivan-driving man looks like a wuss, but whenever I see a guy in a big-ass chromed-out SUV with low-profile tires, all I can think is "tiny penis" (and if he has a pair of TruckNutz swinging from his trailer hitch, "micro penis"). If I were the Hubs, I'd rather look like a wuss than a guy with a tiny penis.

It seems like every week another neighbor comes wheeling into the neighborhood in a flashy new minivan. Everywhere I look, moms are sporting new rides. Every time I see one, it takes all of my self-restraint not to chase it down and carjack it at the closest four-way stop. I drool a little when the proud new minivan owners show me how effortlessly they can program their GPS or fold the back seats flat. So it's no surprise that the minivan conversation comes up over and over.

The last time, we were sitting in our crossover car. (The Hubs made us trade in the SUV because it was a gas guzzler and instead forced a boomermobile crossover car on me. Apparently a minivan is wussy, but driving a car your mother-in-law wants to drive as well isn't emasculating; that's just being fiscally responsible, which is always manly. All I know is my hair gets grayer every time I drive it.) We were on the school pickup line surrounded by happy minivan drivers, and the Hubs said disdainfully, "Really? You really want to drive one of those things?"

"Of course."

"But why? Our car is so much better."

"No it's not! Old people drive this car."

"No they don't."

"Yes they do. In fact, my mom wants to buy one now, because she likes it so much. My *mom*. Look around you—do you ever see anyone under the age of sixty driving this car?"

"Well, no, but that's only because people are sheep. They all want to drive big SUVs and minivans."

"Because they're practical for our lives! A minivan makes sense for us."

"Ugh. They're so . . ."

"They're so what?"

"I dunno. So . . ."

"Oh!" I said, finally realizing his real problem with minivans. "You think you're *better* than a minivan, don't you?"

"So what if I do?"

"Well, you're not."

"I might be," he tried.

"You're not."

"True, but a minivan . . . ugh!"

"What's so bad about it?"

"So many things. First of all, I hate to carpool, and by driving a small car I never have to carpool. Second of all, do you have any idea how much gas would cost? Driving a minivan is like driving a bus. Not this car! I like this car. It's zippy!"

"This car isn't zippy. It's dippy."

"Okay, how about this? Driving a minivan is like waving a sign that says, 'I've given up.'"

"Wow. You're *such* an asshole."

"Pretty much," he agreed. Then he turned and faced me. "But if you really want one, I'll get you one."

He may be an asshole, but he's *my* asshole.

AM I SUPPOSED TO BELIEVE A FIVE-YEAR-OLD MADE THAT?

When I was growing up, my parents were always available to help me with my homework. My dad would explain a complicated math problem to me or quiz me on my spelling words. When I had a report due, my mom took me to the library and helped me navigate the card catalog and the blasted Dewey Decimal System. Even though I had lots of help, never once did they actually *do* my homework for me. My mom never shoved me out of the way and finished my First Thanksgiving diorama, and my dad never wrote my essay on *Hamlet*.

Now that I have kids, I'm noticing more and more parents doing their kids' homework. I don't know about the upper grades, but it's out of control in the lower elementary grades. You only have to walk through the halls of your local elementary school to see the evidence. The bulletin boards are full of some beautiful work done by my peers instead of my children's peers.

When Gomer was in kindergarten the kids were sent home with a paper gingerbread doll. The homework assignment was to use whatever they wanted (except uncooked pasta, because it attracts vermin and the teachers hate mice more than lice) to decorate the little doll and make it "them." The instructions were to take their time, be creative, and really make it unique to the child and his passions. I sat Gomer down and we talked about what he wanted to do with his doll. In those days he was very much into pirates, so he wanted to make his doll a pirate. I thought it was a great idea. I gave him crayons, markers, glue, ribbon, yarn, scissors, and other assorted craft remnants and put him to work at the kitchen table while I made dinner. I checked in on him to see how things were going. A couple of times he stopped to ask for help. Once he asked me to cut a piece of yarn that was being stubborn, and the other time was to take that yucky dried-up glue bit off the top of the bottle so he could work it.

After a half hour my kitchen table and the floor around it were trashed and Gomer had a scurvy pirate with a mess of yarn hair in his one good eye. It was wet with an excessive amount of glue, so it was curling and bubbling a bit. He called me over for a closer look. Earlier I'd been giving myself a pat on the back for being such a good, hands-off mom who let Gomer make his gingerbread doll the way *he* wanted to, but now that I looked at it, I worried that maybe I should have stepped in a bit.

"Is there any glue left, buddy?" I asked.

"A little bit. I wanted to make sure everything stuck," he said.

I looked at my kitchen table. It appeared that my place mats might have gotten hit in the crossfire and were now glued to the table as well. I tried to ignore the mess and concentrate on his gingerbread doll. "Ooh, you made him some clothes, huh?"

Gomer had made some scraggly-looking clothes from scraps of paper and ribbon. His pirate looked like he'd barely survived a shipwreck.

"He's got an eye patch, too!" Gomer said proudly, pointing out the wonky patch that was almost as big as the doll's head.

I thought it looked pretty good for a five-year-old and blunt scissors. That's when I noticed that he had wielded those blunt scissors with wild abandon and cut off one of his doll's legs, gluing on a Popsicle stick in its place to make a peg leg.

"Gomer, you cut off his leg?" I asked, worried. I wasn't sure he was supposed to take it to such extremes.

"Of course I did. It's Pirate Gomer! *Arrrgh!* You can't be a pirate with both legs," he explained.

"I guess so, but I would think you would want to make Pirate Gomer look a little bit like the *real* Gomer. The real Gomer doesn't have a peg leg."

"No, I wanted to make him like a pirate. My teacher said we could do whatever we wanted. That's why I gave him tattoos, too," Gomer said, pointing out the tiny skull-and-crossbones tattoos that covered the body.

Standing back and looking at Gomer's pirate, I got a little nervous. Nowadays the news is filled with stories of kids being sent home because they chewed their peanut butter and jelly sandwich into the shape of a gun or they menaced a teacher. What would the teacher think of Gomer's heavily tattooed, one-legged pirate brandishing a tinfoil sword?

I glanced at the clock. It was way past dinnertime, and I had a mess to clean up before we could even sit down to eat. If I didn't get dinner on the table shortly, my whole nighttime routine would be thrown off, and *I* don't do well when *my* nighttime routine doesn't go according to plan. I had a full DVR of shows to watch and that wasn't going to get done if I didn't get these kids fed and in bed. I decided I didn't have time to help Gomer redo his pirate. I figured the instructions never said he couldn't be a pirate. If the school thought it was a violent choice, I'd deal with the repercussions at that point, because right then I was too exhausted to worry.

In the morning, Gomer carefully packed Pirate Gomer into his folder and proudly brought him to school. I waited with bated breath all day for the phone to ring and to hear the teacher say, "Um, hi, Gomer's mom? Yeah, we have a situation with Gomer and his pirate. Do you have some time to talk?" But the phone call never came. When Gomer came home he told us that his teacher loved everyone's gingerbread dolls.

A few weeks later the Hubs and I were up at the school for parent-teacher conferences. We arrived a little early, and the teacher was still meeting with the family before us. We passed the time by walking up and down the hallways looking at the kids' work. We got to a bulletin board full of gingerbread dolls.

"Hey, look, it's the gingerbread dolls," the Hubs said.

I looked at the bulletin board he was pointing to. The dolls looked really good. "I don't think that's the kindergarten's board," I said.

"You don't?"

"No. Look how great those look. They've got to be older kids." We kept walking closer.

The Hubs got there first. "I don't know. Isn't that Pirate Gomer up there at the top?" he asked.

I looked carefully. He was right. There was Pirate Gomer in all his wrinkled glory, right under the brightly colored header at the top of the bulletin board that said KINDERGARTEN GINGER-BREAD PEOPLE.

"That *is* his," I said, shaking my head. "That's weird. These look so good. I would have never guessed that was the kindergarten's board."

I took a closer look at the gingerbread people surrounding Gomer's dilapidated marauder.

Arrrgh you fucking kidding me? I thought.

My kid's doll looked like it was the only one actually made by a five-year-old. The doll next to him wore a miniature Kansas University cheerleading costume cut and sewn from fabric. Another doll was a ballerina with a tulle tutu and a sequined bodice and neatly braided yarn hair. A doctor in a tiny white lab coat with a minuscule badge clipped to his lapel gazed at me through itty-bitty wire-rimmed glasses. One child's smiling, laminated face was cut into a perfect circle and glued expertly on the head of his cowboy gingerbread doll, complete with fringed chaps and tiny pistol. (So much for me worrying Gomer's doll was too violent; you couldn't even tell the mangled piece of foil on the pirate's belt was a sword, but there was no mistaking the cowboy's pistol.) Every doll I looked at had a perfectly drawn face. No one had a slash for a mouth and a missing nose like Gomer's, and everyone except his had two legs.

I felt my blood pressure rise. *The hell these dolls were made by five-year-olds!*

It was so obvious that the moms and dads sent the kids out to play and then created these mini-masterpieces. At that point I was so torn. On one hand, I wanted my kid's doll to look good, too (and I could have made that little pirate rock), but on the other hand, did I really want to start doing Gomer's homework for him at age five? What kind of parenting is that?

Why would a parent do that? Was it a laziness thing? Were the parents watching the clock and thinking, *Oh crap, it's going to take her an hour to do it and I don't have time to supervise this, but I could knock it out in fifteen minutes, so I'm just going to do it. Shove over, Aighmey, it's Mommy's turn.* Or was it a perfection-ist thing? I could just imagine the overachieving mother sitting there thinking, *Oh God! I can't keep watching him glue his buttons in such a messy line—they must be orderly! Put down the glue and move away slowly, Calvyn!*

No way am I ever going to do my kid's homework. I did my homework time, thank you very much, and the *hell* I'm going to do that again. Besides, I'm way too lazy to actually do his home-work. And what do you do when you've got more than one kid? Who has time for that crap when I've got a new season of *Survivor* to watch?

Call me crazy, but I like to see what sort of stuff my kids can create. I feel like this is what they're supposed to be learning. Sure, it's frustrating to sit there and watch Gomer cut off the leg of his doll or cover its body in tattoos, but it's his doll and he's supposed to be doing it the way he wants to.

So while I was able to hold on to this perspective for a while, I hit a roadblock when Gomer was in third grade. It was about an hour before bedtime when Gomer came to see me, visibly upset. "What's the matter, Gomer?" I asked.

"I forgot to do something," he said.

"Okay, well, you've still got some time before bed. What did you forget to do?" I asked, thinking it was a permission slip he needed me to sign or brushing his teeth.

"I have a research paper due tomorrow."

"A what?" I asked.

"A research paper. It's our first one."

"I'm confused," I said, not really confused. "Why am I just hearing about this now?"

" 'Cause it's due tomorrow."

"I get that. But when was it assigned? I doubt it was today."

"Ohhh. Yeah. No, she told us on Friday that it was due Wednesday."

"So you had the whole entire weekend to work on this and yet you decided to wait until Tuesday night to tell me?"

"I didn't think it would take that long," Gomer whined. "Plus, I had soccer." I guess those two hours of soccer really ate into his research paper time over those two full days off from school.

"Gomer, the whole reason she gave you so many days to do it is because research papers take a lot of time."

Gomer looked like he was going to cry. "There's more," he said.

I sighed. "What else, Gomer?"

"I forgot the book that we're supposed to use for the research part."

Before I could yell, "Are you freaking kidding me?" I had a flashback of my mother yelling at my ten- or eleven-year-old self. She'd just returned from back-to-school night where the teacher had said something about how the parents must be tired of helping with the huge research paper everyone was working on, but luckily it was due the next day and life could get back to normal. My mother watched in horror as everyone around her nodded their heads and she realized she had no idea what the hell he was talking about. I had never once mentioned a looming research paper. Not because I didn't need any help, but because I'd completely forgotten about it. Shit. Of all the qualities Gomer could inherit from me he got my uncontrollable cowlicks and my ability to space out about important shit.

I knew yelling at him wasn't going to help. I couldn't let him fail. I might be an underachiever, but I refused to pass that quality on to him as well! I was going to have to help him.

This was the first time he'd ever had to do a research report, and he didn't know where to begin. We worked through the instructions together. He had to find out facts about three different cities and write a letter home telling his parents about traveling to these cities by train. Since he forgot his book, we had to enlist the help of the Internet (thank God I didn't have to put on pants, go to the library, and try to master the Dewey Decimal System again). He found his facts and started writing his report. Even with Google and high-speed Internet it seemed to take an eternity for him to find the facts he wanted to use. "Mom, what's more interesting? The fact that New York City is home to over eight million rats or the fact that New York City used to be the capital of the United States?" I wanted to yell, *Stop looking at pictures of giant rats and do your work!* In the end he decided to go with capital of the United States, but that was only after reviewing all of the known data on New York City rats. Ewww.

The final instruction was to either handwrite your report super-duper neatly in ink or type it. Gomer had never typed a report before and the idea intrigued him. I suggested he write it all on paper first to get his thoughts in order and then type from the paper.

Once he had his notes scribbled on a scrap of paper he was ready to type. I looked at the clock. It was fifteen minutes before bedtime. Remember what I said earlier about messing with my bedtime routine? *Downton Abbey* was calling me from my DVR and I was starting to get twitchy. "Gomer, do you even know how to type?" I asked him.

"Yes. We're learning to touch-type. I can type twenty-five words per minute," he said proudly.

"Uh-huh," I said, weighing my options. If he didn't type it, he would still have to rewrite his report neatly with ink, and the chances of him screwing up a word here or there and having to start over were high. At least on a computer he could backspace and fix it. I decided to let him type.

When you can type 90 WPM, it is excruciating to sit and watch your child hunt and peck. It was all I could do to not rip the laptop from his hands and whip out his report in three minutes flat. I had to leave the room. "Let me know when you're done, Gomer, and I'll proof it for you," I said.

An hour and a half later he found me, and he was in tears. "What's the matter, Gomer?" I asked, a bit alarmed.

"It's only half a page!" he wailed.

"Okay, so what?"

"The instructions say it must be one page long!" he said, waving the paper in my face.

"Okay, so now we edit and fluff a bit," I told him.

"What does that mean?" he sniffed.

I took the laptop from him. We were an hour past bedtime and I couldn't wait five minutes for him to find the damn *g* key. "You dictate, I'll edit," I said.

The first thing I did was double-space the page, because everyone knows "one page" means "one page double-spaced."

"There," I told him. "That helped. Now we need to expand your paragraphs some more. What else can you tell me about Washington, D.C., that you haven't already told me?"

He thought for a minute and then gave me a random fact about Washington that I've already forgotten, because I'm not the one being tested on this shit.

We worked like that for about fifteen minutes and got his report to the required length.

The next morning as he placed his report carefully into his folder he said, "My teacher is going to love this report!"

"Yup, I think she'll like it," I said, helping Adolpha get on her coat.

"I'm so lucky I have a mom who is a writer. She writes the best reports!"

Adolpha and I both stopped what we were doing and stared at him. "You did Gomer's homework?" Adolpha gasped.

"No!" I exclaimed. "Gomer, I didn't write your report. You did!"

"Not really, Mom. I only wrote half of it and you wrote the other half. The fluffy stuff," he said.

"Not true, Gomer! I just typed and helped you think of some ideas, that's all. The words aren't mine, they're yours."

"Mom, I can't lie to my teacher. You wrote half of my report."

"Gomer! You can't tell your teacher that I wrote it," I said.

"You *did* do Gomer's homework," Adolpha wailed. "You never do my homework!"

I was becoming flustered. "Adolpha, stop it. I didn't do Gomer's homework!" I turned to Gomer. "*You* wrote that report—writing is not typing. *You* did the research and *you* found the facts you wanted to use. You then spent an hour and a half typing it. When it was time to edit it—and by the way, all writers need someone to edit them—I read through it and found the holes you needed to fill. I pointed them out to you and you found more details to add. All I did was type the edits for you because you suck at typing and I couldn't stand to watch you type any longer. You are good at many things, but typing is not one of them. I don't know who's telling you that you can type twenty-five words a minute, but they're lying to you."

"I don't know what you're worried about. My teacher says she likes to read what you write. She's going to be excited to read your report." He turned and walked out the door.

Shit. He was going to throw me under the bus with his teacher, and I didn't even deserve it. The worst part was that I'd be taking a fall for a report that sucked. I mean, honestly, if I had really written that report, it would be outstanding and I would have totally gone with the rat angle. Eight million rats in New York City alone? And what about Washington, D.C.? It would be too easy to write something like, "Rats may be a problem for New York City, but they are the scourge of our great nation's capital. Some are four-legged, but the worst are the two-legged ones." Tell me that's not good stuff right there!

No, none of us can afford for me to do my kids' homework. Gomer and Adolpha will never get into college if they have to rely on me to do their homework. I can help out until about fourth grade, and then they're screwed. I really need these kids to do their own work, because while I can do a badass puppy princess gingerbread doll, when they get to geometry they're on their own.

CARPOOL LINES AND BUNNY PAJAMAS GO TOGETHER LIKE . . . NOTHING. THEY DON'T GO TOGETHER AT ALL.

I tease the Hubs a lot, but really he is the best husband I could hope for. He does a lot of things for our family that I despise doing. Besides putting up with my shit, the most important thing he does is drive the kids to and from school 90 percent of the time. The best part about this is it gives me a good twenty minutes of alone time, when I can have my quiet and empty house to myself. We work together. At home. All day. With no one else. So I live for these twenty minutes of solitude every day. They're honestly the best part of my day.

As much as he tries to schedule his appointments around the drop-off and pickup times, there are times the Hubs just can't make it and I'm the one who has to go get on that dreaded school pickup line. I fuck it up every single time.

One day when Gomer was in kindergarten, he was invited to go and play at his friend Braxton's house down the street after school. Braxton rides the bus, and Gomer does not. I don't really like the idea of my kids riding the bus. I'm a weirdo like that. Call me crazy, but I think that a vehicle designed to transport children should have seat belts. I like my kids strapped into their hard-core five-point-harness car seats in my car. So I told Braxton's mother that I'd bring Gomer over after the bus arrived. (I know, I know, there were much easier scenarios for this, like I could pick up both boys and bring them to her house, but since I don't have a minivan I can't do that, now can I?)

Adolpha was sick and had stayed home from preschool that day. She was a little feverish and pretty clingy, and with Daddy out at work appointments all day, she was looking for lots of love. I'd spent the better part of the day cuddling with her in my bed and watching endless episodes of *Olivia*.

Because I am rarely the one who picks up the kids, I wasn't watching the clock. Suddenly I realized school was going to let out in two minutes and we needed to get Gomer.

I screamed, jumped out of bed, brushed my teeth (yes, I had not yet done that), and grabbed a hat. I bundled up Adolpha and out the door we went.

In our pajamas.

Yes, I knew we were in our pajamas. Well, I only knew because Adolpha said, "Mama, we're still in jammies! We can't go like this!"

I replied, "It's okay, Adolpha, we're just going to drive through the pickup line and grab your brother."

"But Mama, it's *soooo* embarrassing!" she wailed.

I've been embarrassing Adolpha from a very young age. I can't imagine what middle school will be like. She'll probably just tell everyone she's adopted.

I glanced at the clock. The final bell had rung three minutes ago. Gomer was outside waiting for us now. We didn't have time for this drama! I threw her in her car seat, buckled her up, and said my famous last words: "It's okay, no one is going to see us."

Ha! I should have listened to the wise four-year-old.

We drove to the school and found the end of the pickup line. It was practically at my house. A representative from almost every family from our school was lined up to pick up someone. I silently cursed both the school district for making the bus so damn expensive, resulting in so many kids needing to be picked up, and the city for not putting in proper sidewalks so my children could walk to school. (Looking back now, I realize that last curse was just a waste of breath, because honestly, was I really going to walk to school with a sick child to pick up my other kid? *Noooo.* Let's be honest, I wouldn't even want to walk to school with a healthy child!)

We inched our way up to the front and finally got to the driveway in front of the school. I scanned the faces of the few children left and could not see my son. I slowed down when I got to where his grade was corralled, and I could clearly see he was not there.

The teacher who was waving the cars through noticed I'd stopped but no one was climbing in my car. She came to investigate the problem. I rolled down the window. "Have you seen Gomer? I don't see him out here," I said.

"Gomer . . ." She thought hard.

"He's in Mrs. Carlson's class," I said.

"Yes, I know. I'm her sub today. I'm trying to think when I saw him last. Now that you mention it, I never saw him come out of the building! Wait right here." She ran inside the school and got the principal. *Oh great,* I thought. I grabbed a random child's coat that had been discarded in the backseat and threw it over me awkwardly so my pajamas were not so noticeable.

The principal came up to the car window and asked, "Everything okay?"

"Gomer's not here," I said.

"Hmm," he said. "That's not like him."

"No. No, it's not."

"Hmm, I wonder where he could be . . ."

I was starting to panic a bit. Where the hell was my kid? Why was everyone acting so calmly when my kid was missing? Do they usually lose kindergarteners? And then I remembered: the playdate. "Are the bus riders gone?" I asked.

"Yes, why?" the principal asked.

"I think Gomer rode the bus home with Braxton. I told him not to, but I'm sure that's where he is. I'd better go so I can meet him at the bus stop." I felt so much better now. I was positive that's where he was. I remembered him chattering at breakfast that morning about getting to ride the bus, and I reminded him that I was going to pick him up. I was sure he'd stowed away on the bus when the substitute teacher wasn't looking. I just wanted to get out of there so I could go meet the bus and confirm my suspicions. I tried to drive away and hide my embarrassing ensemble, but the principal wasn't having it.

"You'd better come in so we can call the bus company. I'd feel better knowing for sure Gomer's on the bus. Just pull over there and park and come on into the school."

Noooooo!

Good God, man, I'm in my pajamas! I screamed inside my head. And I wasn't in "loungewear" pajamas that could easily pass for yoga pants or something like that. I was in full-on fleecy jammies with matchy-matchy top and bottom. Pink with black bunnies. There was no mistaking what I was wearing.

I looked around. A crowd was starting to form. All I could see was a sea of skinny jeans, ankle boots, blanket sweaters, and Dolce and Gabbana sunglasses. I could see perfectly lined and glossed lips whispering to one another: *Gomer's missing! Why won't his mother get out of the car with the principal? What's wrong with her?*

Now I was frantic to get away. I couldn't let the Dolce moms see me in my fleecy jammies. I didn't have *much* of a reputation to uphold. I'm usually up at the school in ill-fitting cargo pants and shirts with permanent food stains across my bosom—it's like a shelf where I can store leftovers I'll never eat. I'm never the well-dressed mom at any event I attend. If I'm going out to a social thing, I tend to throw on a scarf to cover the stains on my shirt that are already there and the new ones I'll surely acquire that night. I have one or two "cute" hats that are supposed to be stylish, but I need to stop wearing them, because I keep cutting my hair shorter and shorter and now I look sort of bald in my hats. The idea of squeezing myself into skinny jeans and toddling around in high-heeled boots is downright laughable, but I could get used to the giant Dolce and Gabbana sunglasses—then I wouldn't have to worry about my raccoon eyes. Nobody expects much from me when I show up everywhere in cargo pants and Crocs, but my kids and I would be social pariahs if my bunnies and I stepped out of the car.

"Could you call the bus company?" I begged. "I'll run over to Braxton's stop and meet the bus. If the bus company says Gomer's not on the bus, you can call my cell."

I glanced at the dashboard clock. If I left now, I'd have just enough time to run home and pull on some clothes before the bus got there. I'd have to get out of the car at the bus stop and see Braxton's mom, who, I was sure, would be in her own fabulous outfit. But I had to leave right *now*!

I tried to start my car, but the principal stopped me. "I'm not really comfortable with that, Jen. I think you should come in so we can call the bus company together," he said. "Just park the car and come on in."

I could feel sweat forming on my upper lip as I watched the Dolce moms watch me. I was going to have to get out of the car and show everyone that I'd come to school in the middle of the day in my pajamas.

Then I had a genius thought! "Well, I have my little girl and she's sick. I can't leave her in the car alone. . . ."

"Oh! I'd be happy to stay with her!" one of the Dolce moms said. *Really? Are you kidding me, lady? Last week I was walking behind you carrying an armful of treats into the school and you let the door slam in my face, and* now *you're willing to help?* She was probably hoping Gomer really had been kidnapped so she'd have a good story for the girls at bunko on Thursday night. *"It was so weird, you guys. She didn't even seem worried he was missing. It was like she knew where he was—because she'd just buried his body!"*

The teachers, the principal, and the Dolce moms all stared at me and waited. I was out of excuses. What else could I do?

"Well . . . okay. Thanks," I said. Shit. I slowly picked up the kid-sized coat, wishing it was a full-length cape. I had just started to climb out of the car and into infamy when the school secretary ran out of the building shouting, "Gomer's on the bus! Gomer's on the bus!"

"Oh, thank God!" one of the Dolce moms screamed. *Did she actually wipe a tear from her eye? Seriously? Come on, lady, it wasn't that dramatic.*

"Great! Well, I better get going so I can meet him at the bus stop." I started up the car. "Thanks, everyone, for your help and concern!" I yelled as I burned rubber getting out of there.

During the two-minute ride to the bus stop I went back and

forth between being mad at Gomer for disobeying me (and subsequently mortifying me in front of his classmates' moms) and being mad at myself for leaving the house in my pajamas: *Really, Jen? Could you be any more of an idiot?*

I had to go past the bus stop to get home, and I could see Braxton's mother standing there waiting. She waved me down as I got closer. "The bus isn't here yet," she said, "but the driver called. Gomer is on there."

"Yes! Thank you. The secretary was able to reach him, too. I just need to run home real fast and then I'll be right back."

"You do? They'll be here any minute. I thought you might want to speak to Gomer."

"I do! I will! I'll be right back!" I sped off. I was tired of trying to hide my bunny pj's from everyone. I was beginning to look absolutely insane.

I ran home and threw on some dirty clothes (because dirty clothes are at least better than fuzzy jammies) and got back to Braxton's bus stop before the bus arrived. Braxton's mother was gone. Instantly I started missing my comfy jammies. *Where did she go? Why did I even change?* I wondered. As soon as Gomer stepped off the bus and saw me he burst into tears. He knew he'd made a mistake and gotten everyone worried. Before I could decide if I should let him go to Braxton's or not, Braxton's mother came out of her house and announced that the playdate was canceled. "We've been exposed to lice!" she announced. "Beatrix has a friend over from preschool, and I just noticed that her friend has lice. Her mother is on her way to get her, but I have to cancel Gomer. Surely you don't want to take that chance?"

She was right. *Lice!* The worst four-letter word of elementary school. "Ugh! We don't want lice," I said, with apparently a little too much disdain.

"You know, lice are attracted to the *cleanest* heads of hair," she emphasized.

"Well, we should be fine, then, because Gomer's hair is disgusting," I replied.

She looked horrified. *God, no one gets my sense of humor,* I thought.

All my worrying about ruining Gomer's social life for the next four years was wiped away by that one change in events. The Dolce moms had a field day with a lice outbreak in their own ranks, and they quickly forgot about Gomer's mom and her bunny pajamas, letting me slide back into obscurity. The next day I went out and spent $100 on assorted yoga pants so now I can lounge and cuddle in peace and look somewhat presentable when I have to pick up my kids at school.

Now if I could just remember to wear a bra . . .

THE HUSBAND INQUISITION

In the immortal words of Monty Python: "No one expects the Spanish Inquisition." Maybe Monty Python didn't expect it, but I think most women across the country do. Surely I am not the only wife who has to go through the Spanish Inquisition with the Hubs whenever I want to leave the house by myself. Please tell me that I'm not alone.

I have had a standing date with my moms' group every Tuesday night ever since I joined the Blue Playgroup. There are many hints for the Hubs that it's Tuesday and my night out with the ladies: (1) it's on the calendar, (2) I shower, (3) I put on clean clothes, and (4) every Tuesday around 4:00 P.M. I announce, "Don't forget, today is Tuesday. I'll be gone tonight. You're in charge of dinner."

Every Tuesday around 4:05 P.M. I get the following response: "Really? You're going out? Again? Didn't you just go last week?"

"Yes, I did go out last week. I got out every Tuesday," I sigh.

"Must be *niiiiice*. Well, what are you guys going to do? Anything fun?"

I don't know what the deal is. I don't know why it makes a

difference to him if I'm going to have fun or not, but it does. And it seems like the more fun I'm going to have, the more irritated he gets. So I tend to reply: "No, not really. We're all getting bikini waxes and root canals. It should be horrible."

"Oh. Yeah, that *does* sound horrible. Why do you even go to this stuff? We could have so much more fun at home. We could watch TV together. I've got a bunch of *Mythbusters* saved up."

"That sounds great, but I really can't stay home. I'm the one who organized this particular Moms' Night Out, so I'm expected to be there early so I can take the first shot of novocaine before the root canals start."

"Hmm . . . okay. What time will you be back?"

"Whenever the professionals say it's safe to drive, but you'd better plan on late."

Even if I told him the truth, I doubt my Tuesday nights would sound fun to him. Especially the ones where we're having a roundtable discussion about the secrets of potty training or when we bring in an expert extreme couponer to tell us how to get an extra 30 cents off milk from Target (actually, the cheap bastard would love that couponing one). I could barely tell him the night we went to the gun range, because I knew he'd want to tag along. (What? Doesn't your local moms' group go shoot a few rounds to blow off steam?) I don't care what the topic is— I would go and listen to a speaker talk about beekeeping if it got me out of the house and allowed me to spend some time with people who don't want anything from me.

Unfortunately, this line of questioning is not just reserved for Tuesday nights. It seems like I have to play Twenty Questions every time I'd like to leave the house without at least one child in tow. If I try to sneak out the door, I get a barrage of questions:

"Where are you going?"

"What time will you be back?"

"What do we *need* at the store?"

"How much will you spend?"

"What am I supposed to do with the kids while you're gone?"

These questions are just for the grocery store. Can you imagine the hoops I have to jump through to go get my hair cut?

I am home all day long with the Hubs, as we both work from our home office. He is my only co-worker, and he's in my space constantly. I love my husband dearly, but there are days I wouldn't be opposed to burying his bludgeoned body in the backyard. Before you send the police to my house, just know that I dream about this sort of thing, but I would never actually go through with it. I'm weak and he's kind of heavy, so I could never drag his ass out to the backyard or dig a grave. I'm not really built for manual labor.

If it's not the Hubs, then the kids come home from school and I can't even pee alone. Every time I turn a corner I'm met with a whine for more food or help tying a shoe.

I'm sorry that I would like to leave the house for a while—*alone*. I don't think there is anything wrong with the fact that I find the idea of perusing the cereal aisle in peace and quiet appealing. I can't be the only one who at times would like to go to the fucking grocery store by myself. I would like to go in the daylight hours when normal people shop, not after 10:00 P.M., like the Hubs would prefer. I would like to go and walk the aisles in silence and get everything on my list without anyone pestering me for Krave cereal (WTF is that stuff, anyway—crack for kids?), toys, and electronics (I'm looking at you, Hubs!).

I listen to his questions and I typically respond with:

"Target."

"Not sure."

"We need milk and cereal."

"Probably fifty dollars, because you're not allowed to leave unless you spend at least fifty bucks."

"Just keep them alive."

And then I get the dreaded response: "I think we should all go."

Nooooooooooooooo! The Hubs always thinks it's a great idea for *all* of us to go to the store together, like some kind of twisted family outing. This is fun for no one except maybe the Hubs. He loves to be together. Only he doesn't. Because inevitably he has some special item he's looking for in the lawn and garden area or the automotive section (even though he doesn't take care of our lawn *or* our vehicles), so he ditches me with a couple of kids melting down in the cereal aisle because I won't buy Krave, while he goes searching for his random, made-up item that we absolutely must acquire right now. I think the real reason he comes along is so he can better monitor what I'm spending. If he's there, he can pull items out of my cart.

I'm not joking. He is *always* watching my spending. Usually he tracks the credit cards from the home computer. He's the Big Brother of my bank card. One year at Christmastime I went out shopping for presents with my mother. After every transaction, he would call me. "What did you just buy at Toys R Us for $246?"

"Presents."

"I see. We needed that much?"

"Yes."

"Okay, well, are you done for the day?"

"No."

"Okay, just make sure we really *need* all of that stuff before you buy it."

"Uh-huh."

Later that day I went to Best Buy to get him a video game for the Xbox. Before I even got to the car, my phone rang. "You bought me a game at Best Buy?" he asked.

"Well, I bought *something* at Best Buy. What makes you think it's for you?" I asked.

"I know what it is and you totally overpaid. Go back and return it. I can get it cheaper online."

"Are you serious?"

"Of course I am. Go and return it. Best Buy's prices are outrageous. You know that."

That was the last year I bought him a Christmas present.

Between the Inquisition and the online snooping, I don't even know why I bother trying to go out alone. It always ends the same way, with me saying: "Never mind. You ruined it. *You* go to the fucking store and take the kids. I'll stay home and enjoy the peace and quiet of you guys being gone!" And then I turn around and *he's* gone to the store by himself and left me alone with the kids! Well played, Hubs. Well played.

WHO NEEDS DR. PHIL WHEN
WE HAVE ADOLPHA?

Am I the only one who has kids who wait to start the most bizarre conversations until we're all trapped in the car?

We eat dinner together every night, and when I ask, "How was your day?" I get deafening silence. Bedtime is not any better. Instead of telling me about their hopes and dreams as I tuck them in, Gomer remembers an important assignment that's due the next day or Adolpha develops phantom leg pains and they both realize how parched they are. You would think these would be the perfect times to stretch their curious little minds.

Nope, not my kids. It's always when we're in the car. On a trip to the grocery store I went into great anatomical detail when sweet five-year-old Gomer asked where babies come from and wouldn't take my standard "Babies come from God" answer. On a quick jaunt to the library, I tried not to laugh and drive off the road when a very concerned and serious four-year-old Adolpha asked me, "Someday will I have a mustache on my 'china, too?" She'd caught a glimpse of me in the shower that morning and was quite disturbed at the state of my "'china," and wanted to know if there was a way to make hers look better.

Her statement didn't surprise me at all. I can always count on Adolpha to keep it real for me and to never sugarcoat anything. She gets that ability from her father. She once drew a picture of me with enormous crow's feet around my eyes. When I asked about them, she replied simply, "I just draw what I see, Mommy." Remind me to never ask her to draw me from behind.

When she was about five years old, we were on a run to the craft store when she decided to give me the cold, hard truth about the Hubs.

"Mommy, where's Daddy?" she asked.

It was a Saturday afternoon in the spring, and like most Saturdays in the spring, the Hubs was out showing houses to clients. "He's at work," I replied.

Adolpha thought for a moment and then asked, "How do you *know* he's at work?"

I was actually a little confused by her question. "Well, because he told me he was going to work when he left the house this morning," I replied.

"No, *how* do you know?"

"Adolpha, I don't understand your question. What do you mean?"

Adolpha was clearly exasperated with my level of density. "I mean *how do you know* he's at work?"

"I told you. He *told* me when he walked out the door," I replied, mimicking her tone. If she can talk to me like she thinks I'm an idiot, I can give it right back.

"No, Mommy. Maybe he *tells* us he's at work and really he's meeting a girlfriend."

I was stunned by her statement. *Holy crap, kid. Where is that coming from? You're five!*

"Adolpha, where would you get such an idea?" I asked.

"Ms. Shauna's husband had a girlfriend," Adolpha said matter-of-factly. Miss Shauna was our neighbor. "And she had to get divorced, because of the girlfriend."

I couldn't believe she knew that. I racked my brain. How in the world did Adolpha know about Shauna's husband's girlfriend? The whole neighborhood knew—most of them before Shauna, even—but I didn't think the kids knew, too.

"Miss Shauna told you her husband had a girlfriend?" I asked. *Jeez, what the hell, Shauna?*

"No. I heard Aston's mommy telling Ava's mommy."

"You shouldn't eavesdrop on adults' conversations, Adolpha!" I said, letting Shauna off the hook.

"I don't know what 'eavesdrop' means!"

"It means you shouldn't snoop on people's conversations."

"I didn't. I was at Aston's birthday party and she was telling Ava's mommy while they passed out cake. Everyone at the party heard them. Then Rex told us his parents are divorced because his daddy had a girlfriend—only it's a different girlfriend than he has now. Rex said his daddy would go on dates with his girlfriend at night when he said he was at work. See? That's why I want to know where Daddy is. Do people go on dates in the daytime?"

I was shocked. Who knew a bunch of little kids could follow the plotline to a suburban soap opera full of deceit and intrigue? *I* didn't even know Rex's dad had a new girlfriend. Man, that guy gets around!

"Maybe you and Daddy will get divorced," Adolpha continued. "Especially if he has a girlfriend."

I needed to get us back on track, quick. "No, Adolpha. I trust Daddy. Daddy doesn't have a girlfriend. He has me." But now, of course, my little brain started clicking and I started wondering . . .

I began to feel an uneasiness in my stomach. Had the Hubs ever said *whom* was he taking out to look at houses today? I couldn't remember. Then I recalled that he hadn't; he'd only said he'd be home late and that he was taking his client to dinner so they could talk about writing up a contract. Come to think of it, there have been a few dinners that were supposed to result in contracts. The buyers always got cold feet or decided to look at more houses. My mind raced to what I considered to be logical conclusions: Rex's dad was always working late but was really with his girlfriend. The Hubs goes to dinner and doesn't write a contract. Shit, *was* the Hubs cheating on me?

It dawned on me that maybe Adolpha knew something I didn't. Had she picked up on something the Hubs let slip that I had missed? A bit of red lipstick on his collar instead of my signature ChapStick? A hint of perfume instead of my Ben-Gay? A long blond hair instead of one of my short gray ones? I didn't want to drag her into my drama, but I had to know.

"Hey, Adolpha . . ."

"Yes?"

"What made you think Daddy has a girlfriend? Have you ever noticed anything?"

Adolpha replied, "No, I don't think so."

"Has Daddy ever mentioned a girlfriend before?"

"No!" Adolpha looked at me like I was crazy to suggest such a thing. *Hey, kid, we're having this conversation because you started it!*

I looked at her wide eyes. Her answer wasn't good enough. Maybe she had seen something but didn't *realize* what she was seeing. A friend's husband used to go on "daddy date nights" with his daughters and they'd always "coincidentally" run into the same single mom (who also happened to be the office bimbo) who just "happened" to be eating at the same restaurant. And the husband, being the gentleman that he is, always invited this woman to join his party. This went on for several months until the oldest son mentioned to his mother one day that it was weird how often they run into the same skank. That's when my friend put two and two together and kicked out his cheating ass. Maybe the Hubs was bringing his lady friend around and the kids didn't even notice!

I tried a different tactic: "Has Daddy ever introduced you to a lady when I wasn't around?"

"No."

"I mean when Daddy takes you places by himself."

"Daddy never takes us anywhere by ourselves. He always wants the whole family to be together."

That was true. The Hubs never takes the kids anywhere alone. *Seriously, would it kill him to take the kids to a movie sometime by himself and give me a couple of hours of peace and quiet?*

I was getting off topic. "Okay," I said, relaxing. "See? Daddy doesn't have a girlfriend. If he did, we'd see him with someone we don't know or he'd talk about her sometimes."

"I don't know," Adolpha said thoughtfully. "I don't think he's at work today. I think he's with Ms. Marlene."

Marlene was a close friend of mine.

"What?" I practically screamed. *Oh, I'll kill that son of a bitch!* "How do you know he's with Ms. Marlene, Adolpha? Why do you think that?"

"Easy. 'Cause she's your prettiest friend. She's a little bit prettier than you, and Daddy would want a pretty girlfriend. Y'know, one prettier than you."

Gee, thanks, kid. We drove in silence the rest of the way to the craft store. My mind was spinning. *Marlene!* She was prettier than me, but not the Hubs's type. *What is the Hubs's type,* I wondered, *besides short, fluffy, and unkempt?*

I called the Hubs a few times on his cell phone and kept getting his voicemail. That's not unusual, though. Whenever we're with a client, we always ignore our phones. If I wanted to get his attention and let him know we had an emergency, I would need to send him a text message. I almost sent one that said, *You cheating bastard, where are you and what are you doing with Marlene?* Instead, I reined myself in and waited for him to come home from whatever "work" he was doing.

When he got home a couple of hours later, I casually mentioned the conversation I'd had with Adolpha. "I had a funny talk with Adolpha today," I said.

"Oh yeah?" he asked.

"Yeah. You're going to laugh when you hear this."

"Okay, let's hear it."

"So . . . Adolpha thinks you're a cheating bastard." I watched his face closely. "Ha-ha, right?"

"That is funny. She's hilarious."

"Yeah, she's a real hoot," I said. Then I changed gears quickly, trying to catch him off guard. I sneered, "Are you cheating on me, you son of a bitch?"

"What?" he exclaimed.

"Do you think Marlene is prettier than me?" I demanded.

"Who?"

"Marlene. Adolpha thinks you spent all afternoon working on Marlene!"

He laughed and said, "Jen, you and Adolpha are both crazy."

"*I'm* certifiable, no doubt, but *she's* crazy like a fox. She's onto you. She's got your number."

"Jen, you can't be serious," he said.

"I might be. I don't know. Adolpha made some good points today. Like Rex's dad was with his girlfriend when he told his family he was at work."

"Jen, you can't think that I'm cheating on you—and not with Marlene."

"Yeah, that's probably true. Marlene is out of your league," I said.

"She is not. I could totally get Marlene if I wanted her," he argued. "But this is what I love about you, Jen. You're always cracking me up with your stories."

He laughed.

I laughed, too—and then demanded to see his cell phone records.

"Come on, Jen! You're really going to check the cell phone bill? You've never cared about it the entire time we've been married. I took over the cell phone bill because you could never be bothered to pay it and our phones kept getting shut off."

"I don't give a shit about that," I replied. "I want to see the log of who you're calling and texting." I've watched enough *Law & Order* to know that the cell phone bill is always where they get their man.

"It's all online." He waved a hand at the computer. "Go ahead and log in and check it out."

"You know that's above my pay grade. I don't know how to do that," I whined. I'm a technological idiot. I can barely log in to check my email, let alone log in to our bill-pay manager thingy.

He sighed heavily and handed over his phone. "That's a lot of work. Just go through my phone history." After I checked all of his incoming and outgoing calls, emails, and text messages, he said, "Satisfied?"

"I'm not sure." I still wasn't convinced. "You're smart. You probably have two cell phones or something like that."

"Jen," he said, getting serious and a bit irritated now, "either you trust me or you don't. Do you really believe Adolpha? What the hell? She's a preschooler with an overactive imagination. This is stupid. We're fighting over an imaginary girlfriend that our daughter dreamed up!"

I thought about it. Sure, he had lots of opportunities to be away from the house "working" and could easily be using that time to cheat on me, but the Hubs could barely afford me and manage my ridiculous demands. There was no way he could handle two women bitching, whining, and nagging at him and making him buy them stuff.

"You're right," I said. "I'm sorry. She made me a little crazy."

"Well, I guess it's nice to know you still care enough to get jealous," the Hubs replied. "And besides, Marlene would not be my first choice among your friends. It would be Allison. She's much prettier."

"Asshole." Of course it would be Allison, with her fake boobs and hair extensions! The Hubs *really* didn't have a chance with her. I smiled. Let him dream. "Let's go put Adolpha to bed and have a chat with her and let her know that Allison is really more your type."

We went upstairs to Adolpha's room and sat down on her bed.

The Hubs started, "Adolpha, why would you say I have a girl-friend?"

Adolpha looked up at him with huge brown eyes. "Because Mommy doesn't love you as much as you love her," she said solemnly. "She only loves you this much." Adolpha pinched her fingers and squinted to look at the minuscule space between them.

The Hubs laughed and nodded. "Yes! That is so true, Adolpha!"

I was shocked. "Adolpha! Why would you say that? That's not true at all." *At least I don't* think *it is,* I thought. True, there are some days that I love him less than he loves me—he can be sooooo annoying—but not *every* day. No, this was completely unfair. I loved the Hubs just as much as he loved me! If I didn't love him, would I put up with all of his ridiculous rules to save energy, money, and time? (FYI, I'm typing this by the window, because he doesn't like lights to be on in the daytime: "There's no need to pay for lights when we've got nature's light for free!" We only eat out when he has a buy-one-get-one-free coupon. Just once I'd like to go to dinner and not have to choose a restaurant based on what's in his coupon keeper. And he complains I use the brakes too much in our car and wear them out. It's true, I like to brake—because I prefer to stop instead of run into the car in front of me. I don't think it's safe to coast along and hope traffic starts moving before I have to apply the brakes.)

Adolpha turned to me. "It's true, Mommy. Girls always break boys' hearts because they don't love them as much as boys love them. It's okay that Daddy loves you more, but . . ." She paused and looked at me with all of the sincerity she could muster. "He might get a girlfriend 'cause you don't love him enough. You need to be careful, Mommy."

I sat there in stunned silence while the Hubs chuckled, kissed her on the forehead, and said, "That is right. Goodnight, my smart girl."

So there you have it: love advice from my five-year-old kid. She basically told me my friends are too pretty and I'd better step up my game a bit and convince the Hubs I love him more or else he just might get a girlfriend.

"I tell you what," I whispered to the Hubs as we left Adolpha's room. "If she'd do the laundry and the cooking and give me two nights off from my wifely duties for reading and writing, I'd consider letting Allison join the family."

"No way," he whispered back. "We can't afford her. Can you imagine how much our electric bill would be when she's done blow-drying all of that hair?"

DO YOU EVER INVITE ME OVER WHEN YOU'RE NOT TRYING TO SELL ME SOMETHING?

If you ever looked at my calendar, you would think that I have a very active social life. I'm super popular. I get invited to a party almost every single week.

I know you're jealous right now, but you really shouldn't be. It's not like I'm being invited out for drinks or over for a home-cooked meal or even to a bunko game. I never get invited to a cocktail party, a murder mystery dinner, a surprise birthday party, or even a loathsome *half*-birthday party. Nope, the only time I'm invited over is when a friend is hosting one of those home shopping parties where some perky housewife-slash-entrepreneur is going to try and sell me a bunch of overpriced shit that I don't need just so she can drive around town in a shiny new car. And that's mostly because I never say no.

That's right. If I'm available, I go every single time. I'm happy to go, and I buy a pizza cutter or a duffel bag or a scented candle. Whatever they're hawking, I'm buying. I am the easiest mark in everyone's phone book. It's not because I'm a sucker. I go because I am the *biggest* perky housewife-slash-entrepreneur who wants a shiny new car. Only I'm not selling lipstick, I'm selling houses, and I want everyone at that party to buy one from me.

The hostess is usually my latest client throwing a shopping party as a housewarming for her new home, and that's why she's invited me. I owe her. She saw that closing statement. She knows how much I made from selling her that house and she figures the least I could do is buy a damn spatula—or fifty. While *I* might think it was hard work putting up with her impossible demands, conducting late-night marriage counseling sessions, and perfectly blending her champagne taste with a Two-Buck Chuck budget, *she* thinks all I did was drive her around and show her a couple of houses and then cash my check. If I want her to refer me to all her friends at her Pampered Chef party, then I'd better show up and bring my credit card—the one with the *big* limit.

I always buy something I can use (who doesn't need more dry dip mixes or tubes of eye cream?), and I weasel my way into her social group. By the end of the year I'll sell a house to someone connected to the hostess *and* enjoy my delicious dip or less wrinkly peepers.

I've been to so many of these parties by now that I have my routine down cold. I like to arrive just a little early so I can be helpful. I rarely know anyone else attending, so I might as well pour drinks or take coats (after all, I do know where the coat closet is). Also, that's when I can get an idea of what the plan is for the night. Are we doing drinks and browsing the merchandise, or will there be a full-on presentation with a hard sell to write my $995 check for my starter kit and begin my future career in skin care *tonight*? Of course, I prefer the parties where you can mingle rather than just sit there and listen to someone talk to you about the miraculous effects of specially formulated viper venom on fine lines, downlines, and success stories. So if I know it's a presentation, I usually hang out at the back and just let the hostess know that I'll need to slip away before it's over, but I always add, "Please hand me that order form, because I need some of that amazing viper venom eye cream before I go."

Sometimes I like to stay for the presentation, just because every now and again I'm lucky enough to be invited to a party that I know is going to be a hot mess and I don't want to miss it. So when my friend Colleen hosted a sex toy party, I made sure I arrived early, made myself a drink, and got a good seat at the front of the room.

I'd never been to a sex toy party before. None of us had. Colleen and I had met Joyce, the sales representative, at an event the month before where she'd spoken to a room full of middle-aged women about embracing our sexuality. During her speech, Joyce never mentioned she was a sales rep for Flaming Desire parties. Instead, she stood there in her buttoned-up business suit and talked to us about harnessing and releasing our "feminine energies," whatever the hell that meant. I guess Colleen understood what she was talking about, because afterward she wanted to meet Joyce and thank her for coming. We finally got close enough where we could shake her hand and promise to be "mindful" of our sexual health. When Colleen confided to Joyce that she wished she could do a better job releasing her feminine energies, Joyce said, "Oh! You and I need to talk!"

Joyce explained that while giving speeches is a fun hobby, her *real* job was selling pleasure. She determined that what Colleen really needed was a good, sturdy vibrator. However, a good vibrator is expensive, and Colleen needed to throw a Flaming Desire party so her friends could buy enough lube and flavored condoms to help offset the expense. Colleen booked a party on the spot.

A few weeks later Joyce arrived at Colleen's house out of breath and lugging a giant suitcase into the front hall. "Hi, sexy ladies!" she called out.

We all looked behind us. Was she talking to us?

I barely recognized Joyce. Sex-toy-sales-consultant Joyce looks very different than embracing-your-sexuality-speech-giving Joyce. One thing I'll say about Joyce is that she fully embraces who she is. She is a big girl with a lot going on, yet she wasn't afraid to pour herself into a tight miniskirt that barely covered her business. She worked her fishnet stockings, which were straining to hold her fleshy legs, and I've never seen a woman with such a large bosom give so little regard to a supportive bra. Her peasant top could hardly contain her enormous breasts, which swung wildly (and I'm pretty sure freely) every time she moved. When she spoke she was incredibly animated and bounced around a lot, using her hands to articulate. When she really got going, I had to avert my eyes, because I was sure there would be a boob escape at any moment.

We moved into the living room and bunched together and tittered like a bunch of schoolgirls while we watched Joyce unpack her suitcase. It was like a clown car at the circus, only the clowns were dildos—each one bigger and more neon-colored than the next, because nothing turns ladies on more than a bright green boner. Besides the toys, she also had tons and tons of "nibblers," as she liked to call them. These would be your edible panties, flavored condoms, and chocolate-flavored dust. Instead of getting me excited, these just made my stomach growl. Colleen had focused a lot on the drinks for the night but hadn't given much thought to the food, and I was starving!

"Okay! Shall we get started?" Joyce asked. "My name is Joyce, and tonight I will be showing you the secrets to unlocking your hot and sexy side!"

Everyone whooped and cheered. "Yeah, sexy!" I yelled, just because I was hangry and felt like being an ass.

"Who's ready to unlock her inner diva?" Joyce cried, waving a dildo around.

"I am!" yelled Colleen. I moved her drink out of her reach. Her inner diva was hammered already.

"Would you believe that just a year ago I was a wallflower who didn't have a date?" Joyce asked.

I looked closely at her bad skin and fried hair. *Yes,* I thought. *Yes, I would believe that.*

"A year ago I was introduced to Flaming Desire parties, and my life has never been the same since. I now date men half my age! Every time I go out to a bar or restaurant I never buy a drink! I have men fighting over me. And this is all thanks to Flaming Desire products."

The whooping and screaming stopped, and we just stared at her. Every woman in the room was married with kids. The last thing we wanted was a bunch of college-age douchebags fighting over us in a bar.

Finally I spoke up. "Yeah, good for you, I guess, except we're all married," I said. "We're not really looking to get free drinks and men fighting over us."

"I hear ya, but wouldn't it be nice to know that men out there still want you?" Joyce winked. "Wouldn't it be great to see your man twitch a little when a drink arrives at your table courtesy of a stranger?"

"I don't understand," our friend Gloria said. "Men will buy me drinks because I use a vibrator?"

"No, silly! Men will buy you drinks because they will recognize you as a sexually liberated woman who knows exactly what she wants! They will sense your aura! The vibrator just helps you unlock your inner diva."

"Ohhh," Gloria said, still confused.

"Hold on," I said. "I couldn't give a shit about my inner diva and free drinks from strangers in bars, and I have a box full of battery-operated fun collecting dust in the back of my closet. Here's what I really want, and maybe you have it in your bag of dicks over there. I want something that will fold laundry and satisfy my husband so he will leave me alone to read my book in peace."

"Amen!" Gloria yelled.

"Oh, that sounds good. Yes, I want that, too," said Colleen.

"What are you talking about?" Joyce asked. "You said you wanted to release your feminine energies."

"Yeah, I don't think so. See, here's the part you don't understand," I explained to Joyce. "We're all married. We have been for years. Our husbands want to have sex with us. All the time. Being desired isn't our problem. We're desired. *Too* desired, in fact. We're exhausted. I don't want to lick chocolate dust off my husband's chest, because that shit will get on the sheets and then that makes more laundry for me. I don't want a giant green dildo, because that's one more damn thing in my house that will need new batteries in a few weeks, and after a while my husband will start to feel inadequate in comparison and then I'll have to pump up his confidence again, which is something I don't have time for. I'm not interested in making my husband want me more. I'm looking for something that will keep him occupied so he'll leave me alone, and if it can wash dishes, too, even better. If you're selling something like that, then I'll buy one for everyone in the room."

Joyce didn't know what to make of me and my friends. I think we were the first bunch of women she'd partied with who didn't want to re-create *Fifty Shades of Grey*. She quickly realized her dream of selling us giant penises and S&M fetish starter packs was over and she was just going to have to focus on the old-lady basics: dry vaginas.

"Well, obviously, I don't have anything like that, but how about lube?" she said. "You can't always get out of the deed, and so for those times wouldn't it be nice to have everything working together smoothly . . . and quickly?"

"Yes, I suppose that would be helpful," I replied, thumbing through her catalog of lubricants. I gasped a little. Who knew lube cost so much more than a spatula?

Joyce must have heard me, because she said, "Jen, did I mention that I'm in the market for a new house?"

I bought the S&M fetish starter pack as a present for Colleen and sold Joyce a lovely three-bedroom bungalow.

SLEEPOVER IS NOT A PARTY THEME! AND OTHER STUPID THINGS SUBURBAN MOMS COMPLAIN ABOUT

You always know when it's back-to-school time. Many suburban moms across the country bump into one another in the school supplies aisle as they're trying to figure out the difference between a poly folder and a plastic folder and cursing the teachers for choosing the large glue sticks when the small ones are the ones on sale. These moms haven't seen one another since the extravaganza/carnival/field day/picnic, and now it's the perfect time to block the aisles with their overflowing carts, ignore their wilding offspring, and catch up on what they've missed.

While I choose not to partake in all this revelry, I always park my cart in the next aisle over so I can eavesdrop, because that's just how I roll.

There's a formula to these conversations. It's always the same endless loop. It goes something like this:

> **Kori:** Jillian! Hi! Oh my God. I haven't seen you all summer.
> Not since you moved to Willow Tree Bend Hills. How is
> the new neighborhood?
> **Jillian:** Oh wow, Kori. Hi! Yes, Willow Tree Bend Hills is

amazing, of course. Are you guys still stuck in Ainsley
Lake Meadow?

Kori: Well, I wouldn't say "stuck." We still like it a lot.

Jillian: Really? You don't think it's weird that there isn't a
lake?

Whit: Well, it's no weirder than the lack of willow trees or
hills in your neighborhood, Jillian.

Kori: Whit! I cannot believe you are here. I thought your
nanny would do the school supply shopping for you.

Whit: I know! I can't believe it, either. She's on vacation this
week. Her mother is having surgery or something. It's
been a *total* nightmare for me. I have no idea why I
allowed her to go. I was so stupid! I haven't set foot in a
big box store in months. I forgot how disgusting they are.

After the neighborhood smackdown comes the faux passive-
aggressive backhanded compliments:

Jillian: Well, even when you're slumming, you still look
great, Whit. CrossFit?

Whit: Hot yoga and eyelash extensions.

Jillian: Did you get the Groupon for the lashes? They look
like the ones I saw advertised last week.

Whit: God, no. I would never go cheap on my eyelashes.
You could go blind if the right person doesn't do them for
you! Was that the same Groupon that was advertising
liposuction, too? I didn't even open that one. I guess you
did, huh?

Kori: It can be frightening to get discounted treatments like
that! They're so sketchy. You don't do that, do you, Jillian?

Jillian: Of course not! I just picked up the one for a chemical peel for Sebastian. He's the only one brave enough to do the discount ones.

Whit: I didn't realize men are getting chemical peels now.

Jillian: Well, mine is. He gets waxed, spray-tanned, and Botoxed. He might as well add chemical peel to his arsenal, too.

Kori: It's more than the lashes . . . there is something else. Your boobs look better than ever.

Whit: *Shhh!* I got them lifted. You guys remember, I had them done as a high school graduation present, but time and gravity had taken their toll.

Jillian: That's it! Well, they look great.

Whit: Not as good as Kori's nose.

Kori: Oh! You noticed! Yes, Phil's gift to me for Mother's Day. I got my chin done, too. Phil never liked it. He always said it was too strong. Whatever that means. It hurt like a bitch, but I think it's a definite improvement.

Jillian: Of course it is! I'd love to get my chin done!

Whit: Just do your boobs. No one is looking at your chin, Jillian.

Kori: So true.

Now that everyone is feeling slightly fat, cheap, and ugly, the conversation finally moves on to school. After all, it's that time of year and it's all anyone can talk about. No mother in my community has a more widely recognized hobby than bitching about her child's school. I've come to realize that for many, school is a real drag. It gets in the way of raising a professional athlete. Really. One of these days I'm going to be surrounded by so many young gifted athletes. There must be something in the water, because everyone's kid is a prodigy of some kind, except for mine.

Gomer is a bit of a lumberer on the soccer field, and when Adolpha practices her ballet, she has the grace of a baby giraffe. They're so like their mother. I couldn't be prouder of my little underachievers.

Whit: So, which teachers did you guys get this year? We've got Monroe and Phillips.

Kori: Oh, Phillips is kind of a bitch.

Whit: She is?

Jillian: Yeah, last year she made the kids do homework every single night.

Whit: What the hell is her problem? It's only third grade!

Kori: We had to have a meeting with her, because between tae kwon do, soccer, diving, and filmmaking Cavanaugh only had one night a week to do homework.

Jillian: Oh I remember that! She was a total bitch to you guys. Didn't she want you to drop everything?

Kori: Yes. As if! How is he going to get into a good college if he isn't well rounded?

Jillian: Exactly. How can you raise a well-rounded kid when the teachers are constantly sending home busywork for them to do?

Whit: Why can't they get everything done during the day? What are they doing all day?

Kori: That's what we wanted to know, too!

Whit: Well, I've got news for her. Tex simply adores baseball, basketball, track, tennis, and oil painting. He won't be dropping out of any of those for schoolwork! I think Brick would have a coronary if I told him Tex couldn't play baseball on three teams this year. Brick's philosophy is that when you join the Yankees nobody asks you what your GPA was in third grade.

Jillian: Well, I think the key is to just set the right tone from the beginning of the year, Whit. Just let Phillips know that you're Tex's mother and you'll do what you think is best. Besides, our tax dollars pay her salary, so it's like she works for us! Don't let her forget that.

Kori: Exactly!

With that crisis averted, it's now time to move on to the second-favorite topic in the suburbs: parties. Ridiculous, competitive, over-the-top parties to celebrate stupid things like potty training or half birthdays or Monday.

Jillian: Hey! While I have you both here. Are either of you going to Casper and Jasinda's gender reveal party?

Whit: Of course! Their gender reveal parties are incredible. Not. To. Be. Missed.

Kori: I don't think I got invited.

Jillian: Really? I thought everyone was invited.

Kori: Maybe I missed the invitation in the mail. I get so many. What did it look like?

Whit: It was hand-delivered by a beekeeper who she heard speak at her Mothers' Night Out. They're doing "What Will It Bee?" as their theme.

Jillian: The theme is a little tired, but I thought they freshened it up. Didn't you, Whit?

Whit: Totally. This guy rang my bell in full-on beekeeping apparel, or whatever you call it. It was adorable.

Jillian: Cutest thing I've ever seen.

Whit: Then he hands you a jar of honey that Casper harvested from their bee colony in their backyard. With the invitation attached.

Kori: Hmm . . . I wonder what happened to our invite. We've gone to their three other gender reveal parties.

Jillian: I don't know. Now that I think about it, you weren't at Mellodee's Earth Day party. Were you invited to that?

Kori: No. I just assumed she didn't do one this year.

Whit: Oh no, she did. It was unbelievable. Every kid got their own sapling to take home and plant.

Jillian: I wonder if this has to do with your neighborhood, Kori.

Kori: What do you mean?

Whit: Everyone hates your neighborhood. We call it Ainsley Lake Ghetto. A gal in my bunko group came up with that. I thought it was hysterical.

Jillian: You should really think about moving, Kori.

Kori: But we all go to the same elementary school. My neighborhood can't be that bad.

Whit: Did you know that we're trying to get the boundaries changed so that you guys won't go to our school anymore?

Kori: What? Why?

Jillian: Because it's so hard on the kids. It's really awkward to go to school with random kids who don't have the same upbringing. Plus, they feel pressure from the administration to branch out and become friends with the Ainsley Lake Meadow kids.

Kori: Same upbringing? We have a lake house and spend our winter break on the slopes in Colorado just like you guys.

Jillian: You're one of the rare ones. Almost everyone else spends their summers in town, and there are kids in Kinslee's class who can't even ski.

Whit: We've all noticed that the Ainsley Lake Meadow birthday parties are very lacking in originality.

Kori: Oh, I don't know about that! We just had Luna's party. It was so much fun.

Whit: What was your theme?

Kori: It was a retro theme. We did an eighties party with a sleepover. Just like we used to do when we were little.

Jillian: See, that's what I'm talking about. Sleepover can't be a theme.

Kori: No, eighties was the theme. We had a rainbow cake, even. It was ironic.

Whit: Did people realize it was ironic or did they just think you were cheap?

Kori: I think they got it.

Whit: I agree with Jillian. If I was going to do an eighties theme, I would make all of the girls dress up like Madonna or Tiffany. I'd rent an entire roller rink and I'd hire professional break-dancers to perform on skates.

Jillian: I would give the girls a DVD of the entire *Mork and Mindy* series and rainbow suspenders in their goody bags.

Whit: I'd give each girl a personalized satin jacket.

Jillian: Love that, Whit! What was in your goody bags, Kori?

Kori: We didn't do goody bags . . . I just think most of that stuff is crap.

Whit: It's only crap if you buy crap, Kori. And Ainsley Lake Ghetto parties are full of crap. This is exactly what we're talking about.

Jillian: Think about it. Luna only turns seven once. Don't
  you want to make it a special day for her? Don't you care
  what others think about her and her party?

Kori: I hadn't thought of it that way.

Whit: It's the only way to think about it. It's not just about
  you anymore. That's why I hire a party planner every
  year. It needs to be spectacular and one of a kind—just
  like your kids.

This is the part where I realize that I've been slowly drifting
out of my hiding place. I've been so mesmerized by Whit's new
boobs and Kori's shitty neighborhood that I've completely exposed myself. I'm now in the middle of their aisle in plain view
of everyone. While I try to pretend a real interest in bevel eras-
ers, I become the subject of their conversation.

Jillian: Oh my God! Look! Isn't that what's-her-name? The
  one who came to school in her pajamas?

Kori: I think it's her. I can't tell. I've never seen her in clothes
  before.

Jillian: I'm pretty sure it's her.

Whit: Of course it's her. Look at her cart. Full of garbage and
  cheap yoga pants.

Jillian: Yeah, those look good on no one.

Whit: They look better than fuzzy pajama bottoms.

Jillian: True.

Kori: Should we say hello?

Whit: Why would we do that?

Kori: I don't know. It just seems like the polite thing to do.

Jillian: Yeah, I guess we could say hello. I'm selling
  Pampered Chef now. Maybe she would throw a party.

Whit: God, you're always selling something, Jillian. Surely she has a few friends that she could invite over.

Kori: I hope they know they should get dressed first.

Jillian: Okay, I *cannot* have pajama lady throw a Pampered Chef party.

Whit: There you go, Kori. Do you want Luna to end up like pajama lady?

Kori: God, no!

Jillian: Then throw her a decent party, for God's sake.

Whit: Look, you've missed half-Christmas, June 25, but August 10 is National S'Mores Day. You still have time. Here's the number for my party planner.

Jillian: Now, let's get out of here before pajama lady tries to speak to us!

IT'S FREE BOWLING, LADY,
NOT THE JUNIOR OLYMPICS

Summers in Kansas can be a bit rough. We have no beaches to escape to and no mountains to climb. We have a bounty of public pools we can jump into on a hot summer day, but there aren't too many options for the rainy days or the way too hot days where you don't want to sit and bake in the sun. On days like these when Gomer and Adolpha were little we used to take their scooters and hit a virtually abandoned mall, where I'd let them fly up and down the desolate corridors in a perfect climate-controlled environment. As they got older (and faster) I realized the liability might be too great if they accidentally mowed down one of the senior citizens on their daily power walk. It was around this time—Gomer was seven, Adolpha was five—that I heard about the free bowling summer program.

Yes, there is such a thing. Every weekday each kid gets two free games at our local bowling alley. You have to pay to rent the shoes, unless you're clever like me and go on eBay and buy the shoes (and then I sell them on eBay the next year when they grow out of them—I told you I was clever). I figure we need to bowl at least five times before our shoes are paid for. We get our money's worth. (Yes, the Hubs's thriftiness has started to rub off on me.) We're there a lot and we always see some *really* interesting people. Usually it's leagues full of elderly bowlers who seem to enjoy the bowling gear more than the actual bowling. Why does every bowler over the age of sixty-five have at least two balls and three pairs of shoes? They also always have fancy wrist protectors or finger wraps. And let's not forget the towels! They have a chamois for everything! One to gently caress the ball with, one to mop the damp brow with, and a backup in case the first two get too grimy. They squawk and squabble with one another about who has the best crap, and even when they're this old, the men are still trying to impress the women with their prowess and flashy junk.

My kids are accoutrements freaks. They see these "pros" and they want that shit, too. Adolpha swears the Barbie bowling ball would make her a better bowler, and Gomer is convinced the finger wrap would help him get strikes every time.

This year we have new management at the lanes, and they realized it was probably a good idea to keep the freeloading kids at one end of the room and the paying customers at the other. This new change has cut down considerably on our interaction with the old folks and our visits to the pro shop on the way out the door.

While I found the aged bowlers fascinating and enjoyed watching their dramas unfold, I'm learning that the kid bowlers have their own drama, too, and it can be just as entertaining.

One hot summer day, I'd taken Gomer to the lanes to cool down and scope out the swag. We were halfway through our first game when a mother-daughter duo showed up and took the lane next to us. As they got settled my son scored a strike. The other mom cheered for him. I smiled at her, but thought, *Oh no.*

We're not going to have to be friendly, are we? I just want to bowl with my kid, and I'm in no mood to make polite chitchat. I suck at that. Needless to say, I didn't need to worry. By the end I was afraid to open my mouth because I try not to swear in front of my kids or give unsolicited parenting advice (at least out loud).

The daughter was about ten and was bowling by herself. Mom was just there for moral support. She'd even brought a magazine and pretended she was going to read it.

The girl bowled her first ball and put it in the gutter. Mom's head snapped up from her *Vogue*. "What happened? Were you not concentrating? Why did you do that?"

"Concentrate?" the girl said. "What do you mean? I'm just throwing the ball."

Mom slowly, deliberately closed her magazine, set it down, and said, "What. Do. You. Mean. You're. Not. Concentrating? Bowling is a game of concentration. Don't you want to be good at bowling? Don't you want to feel good about yourself when you accomplish a high score?"

WTF? It's free summer bowling, not the Junior Olympics.

The girl said, "I really don't care. It's just bowling."

"Well, you should care. That little boy next to us is beating you. He's probably like five and he's beating you. How does that make you feel?"

At this point I looked at my phenom bowler (who was actually seven at the time) to see if he was hearing this conversation. Apparently I'm the only Nosy Nellie in the family, because my kid was oblivious. Thank goodness, because I really didn't want to have to tell this woman to pipe down, and if it bothered my kid, I was going to have to.

The mom never picked up her magazine again. She continued to berate and "coach" this little girl until it was absolutely uncomfortable to watch (but I managed to, of course). "Oh come on, *another* gutter ball? That little boy hasn't had one yet." (Yeah, that's because that little boy was playing with the bumpers up; he would be pretty freaking fantastic if he could manage to get a gutter ball.) "Concentrate! I can tell you're not concentrating. Do it right this time. . . . See! You just got a spare. Doesn't it feel good to be a winner? Don't you want to feel like that all the time?"

Seriously, lady? What is wrong with *you*? Does everything need to be a competition? Does your kid need to win *everything* she does? Is winning the only way for her to develop self-worth?

I got the impression this little girl is an only child, so right there is a ton of pressure on this kid, and then you add a mom who makes her feel like crap because a seven-year-old was beating her at bowling (with bumpers, don't forget) . . . yeah, I think that's probably a recipe for an eating disorder. Free bowling is just for fun; can you imagine what real organized sports looks like in this family?

Probably a lot like some of the kids' games I've been to. I don't know what it is about this town, but everyone is positive they're raising the next A-Rod or Nadia. The parents spend an absolute fortune on bats and mitts and private lessons and camps and tournaments, all so their kids can be called winners. I don't see these same parents signing their kids up for Mathletes or chess club. It's always baseball, football, dance, gymnastics. They put all of this pressure on their eight-year-old kid to succeed and win at any cost. I've been to soccer games where dads are yelling, "Take him down, Jefferson! Just like I showed you! Make sure he can't get back up!" and gymnastics classes where the star falls off the balance beam and the moms hold their collective breath while calculating just where their precious child would fall in the lineup if Ms. Thing is severely injured.

There has got to be a better way to motivate your kids. Of course I want my kids to be successful, too, but I feel like I have to pick my battles. I'd like for Gomer to practice his soccer and stick with it. He enjoys it and he's a decent soccer player. I don't expect him to win every game, and I fully expect him to come home someday and tell me he wants to try another sport.

Adolpha isn't sure what she wants to do. We've tried dance, but she is her mother's daughter (i.e., graceless). Cheerleading was not a hit: "What am I doing here, Mommy? I'm freezing cold and I'm cheering for a bunch of boys to win a game! Who cheers for *me*?" (Exactly, Adolpha. Exactly.) Soccer requires way too much running, but she loooooves the kick-ass socks. (I told you my kids love the "gear.") Now she thinks she'd like to try basketball, mostly because she's tall and she thinks high-tops are cool. (Sigh. More gear.) After one broken arm and multiple mishaps, I'm thinking my klutzy daughter might be better off in art classes.

Good thing for us the mother-daughter duo finished up their games before we did or else Mom would have totally schooled me—I barely beat Gomer in the first game, winning by just ten pins, and in the second game he destroyed me. I obviously lost my concentration once they arrived, and I couldn't get my head back in the game. Stupid! Stupid! Stupid! I won't let that happen again! I felt like crap that night. I almost binged and purged.

I THOUGHT MOTHER'S LITTLE HELPER WAS A BABYSITTER. I WAS WRONG— IT'S DRUGS.

I've always been a little naive when it comes to drugs. I've never tried them and I don't know many people who use them. When I was in college, some friends and I drove across the country to attend the Woodstock '94 concert in upstate New York. As we were driving down the highway, a carload of boys pulled up beside us. The passenger held up a handwritten sign that said, GOT A BOWL?

"Why do they want a bowl?" I asked my friend. "Are they making a salad?"

My friends teased me mercilessly because it took me several more exits to realize they weren't making a salad—or soup.

So it's no surprise that it took me so long to figure out that I'm one of the few moms in my town not on drugs. When I say drugs, I don't mean pot or meth. I mean the good stuff: Valium, Adderall, Oxy. I'm the only one left who's feeling my feels and suffering from wild mood swings. I'm the only one who can't remember to pick up the kids at school when they have half days. I'm the only one who leaves the house in my pajamas because I can't get my shit together, nor do I give a shit that I can't get my shit together. I'm the only one whose house is constantly buried in piles of laundry, and I am the only one who never makes homemade anything for class parties. (Hey, someone's got to bring the paper products, and I am happy to be that mom.) When I go to the grocery store, I'm surrounded by perfectly put-together Stepford wives with fake smiles and dead eyes searching for the best organic food to put into their bodies as a chaser for their drug cocktails. (Am I the only one who finds it ironic that they won't eat a Cheeto, but they have no problem downing narcotics like they're Tic Tacs?)

I know, I know—for many of these women, these drugs are a necessity. They cannot leave their houses without their Zoloft and their Xanax. Those are not the women I'm talking about. I'm talking about the tons of women who pop pills just to smooth out the sharp edges, help them focus on their staggering to-do lists, or dull the boredom of their lives. These are the women for whom these drugs aren't a daily necessity to function in the world; instead they're the ones who use them as mother's little helpers.

I'm so stupid, I always thought a mother's little helper was a young neighbor girl who babysat your kids for a pittance while you ran some errands. When I was nine years old, I was sometimes hired to be a mother's helper. I was paid a quarter an hour to sit in a house with a neighbor's sleeping baby and watch TV. My only job was to make sure to get the baby safely out the door if the house somehow caught on fire.

Being a mother's helper really sucked. The pay was terrible and the baby had a sixth sense that would make her wake up as soon as her mother left. So instead of watching TV I was forced to shush an irate baby for a lousy quarter.

I've since realized that I was wrong. No one works for a quarter anymore, and now mother's little helpers aren't neighbor girls—they're drugs. No wonder the supermoms can accomplish so much in twenty-four hours! I could get a lot done, too, if I was jacked up on Adderall and Vicodin.

These doped-up supermoms are the ones who turn every children's soccer game into a pharmaceutical black market. You can always spot them, because they look like a bunch of tweakers pushing up on one another looking for their next fix. They say stuff like, "I just used my last Xannie and I can't get in to see my doctor until Tuesday. Do you have one you could spare? It's been a *day*."

As intense as these women are, they seem fairly harmless compared to the superusers. I've only met one superuser. Adolpha broke her arm when she was five, and it required surgery. She was prescribed something fairly heavy-duty to numb the pain and help her sleep. After a few weeks, I received a text message from a mom I know (aka the superuser).

Superuser: How is Adolpha feeling?

Me: Much better, thanks.

Superuser: Oh good! Did they give her anything for the pain?

Me: Yes, we have a prescription to help her sleep, but she stopped needing it a week ago. Tylenol is doing the trick now.

Superuser: Oh good! Any chance she has any leftovers I can buy from you? I have a terrible migraine and I could use something to help.

I was stunned. I wanted to write back: *What the fuck, lady? Did you just offer to buy my child's pain meds?*

I chose not to respond to the text. I just ignored it. Then a few days later I got another one.

> **Superuser:** I don't know if you got my last message. I need to buy Adolpha's leftover pain meds. I've got an awful toothache and I can't get to the dentist this week. My dentist would totally prescribe something for the pain, but I just can't get there, so it's just easier if I pay you for Adolpha's. Would fifty bucks work?

I ignored her again. I didn't know what to do. Luckily, she wasn't someone I see on a regular basis, so at least I didn't have to see her in the parking lot at school and have her ask me face-to-face to sell her drugs illegally. After another few days passed I received the final text message from her.

> **Superuser:** Hey, just so you know, I was totally kidding about buying Adolpha's meds. It was just a joke. You can stop being all weird and judgy now.

That's when I took superuser out of my phone. I'm not interested in being friends with a fucking junkie.

I'd rather be friends with the supermoms. Sure, they're on drugs, but at least they're not downing cherry-flavored cough syrup to get high. I don't want to get high. I just want to get my shit together. I need the supermoms to fill me in. I'm so pissed off that they won't let me in on their secrets. I just want to know if it's a blue pill or a white pill that makes you bake *ah-may-zing* brownies, or if it's a red pill or a yellow pill that gives you the stamina for a two-hour workout. I've tried to ask subtly, but no one will 'fess up. Those bitches will never let me in their club. I finally decided to confront the next supermom I met and just simply ask her.

It was a beautiful fall day at the soccer fields when I met Stacy for the first time. The game had just begun when she arrived carrying homemade pumpkin spice muffins with cream cheese frosting for everyone, photos of the jack-o'-lantern she had elaborately carved earlier that morning into the shape of a witch stirring a bubbling cauldron with the rising steam spelling out the word "Boo," enough material and glue for each of the siblings not playing soccer to make adorable "easy no-sew" bat wings as a fun craft to fill their time, as well as little gift bags for every mother full of Halloween-themed wine charms and sleep masks that were embroidered with "Sleeping for a spell." Besides her generous gifts, she also looked terrific. She was wearing the perfect fall outfit with just the right number of layers and textures and cool boots. Her hair was beautifully twisted into a loose braid casually thrown over one shoulder. While everyone sat in their lawn chair and screamed at their kid to "attack the ball," Stacy ran up and down the sidelines taking (no doubt fabulous) photos of her son and overseeing the siblings' craft bonanza.

At this point I should also mention, in case you don't feel bad enough about yourself, that Stacy has a full-time job outside the home. Like a really important one. I'm not sure what she does exactly, but from the thirty seconds that she slowed down long enough to talk to me, I learned that she works fifty hours a week or so and travels around the country every few days and then comes home and makes her kids pancakes in the shape of clovers for breakfast, because it's International Clover Day or some shit like that. When I told her I was surprised she knew it was International Clover Day, she informed me that every day should be a holiday. She told me there is an international holiday of some kind almost every day that you can celebrate. (She's absolutely right! I just looked, and today is the day the French celebrate the anniversary of the execution of Marie Antoinette. Maybe I should make hot dogs for dinner tonight and design a tiny razor-sharp guillotine to cut them into bite-sized pieces.)

After thirty seconds with her I was wiped out. "Okay, seriously, I have to know, Stacy. How do you do it all?" I asked her as I bit into one of her delicious muffins. *Damn!* I thought, *I don't even like pumpkin, and these are fucking awesome!*

"You just have to prioritize, Jen," Stacy advised me. "I'm a *huge* list maker."

"*Riiiight.* List making," I said. I didn't buy it. "Come on, Stacy. I know there's a secret. I know that all of you perfect moms are on drugs. I just want to know which ones so I can get on them, too. You guys are so secretive and keep that shit to yourself. Is it Adderall? What do I have to tell my doctor to get him to prescribe some for me? Every time I tell him I'm tired or distracted, he tells me to try yoga. *Fucking yoga!*"

"Excuse me?" Stacy stopped taking pictures and looked at me, horrified. "Are you suggesting that I'm a drug addict or something?"

The rest of the moms around us went silent. "Well . . . I just . . . ," I stammered. "'Drug addict' sounds kind of harsh. It's not like you've ever tried to buy my kid's leftover Oxy or anything."

"What in the world are you talking about?" Stacy asked.

"Nothing. Look, I just want some pep in my step, too," I whined. "I want what you have. Is it Ritalin? It's Ritalin, right?"

"My *daughter* takes Ritalin," Stacy gasped.

"I figured it was Ritalin," I heard a mom behind me whisper.

"And you don't swipe a pill from her here or there?" I asked Stacy.

"Of course she does," the mom behind me whispered.

"Who wouldn't?" another chimed in.

"Absolutely not! Jen, I'm sorry that you can't get your life organized and that you can't seem to find the time to do nice things
for yourself and your family, but that doesn't mean that just because *I* can, then I must be a drug addict! Now, as I told you earlier, I have a very high-powered and stressful job, so of course
there are times that I take a nerve pill or two to help me get
through an important day, but I'm not one of those stay-at-home
moms downing Xanax all day. *They* are the ones with a problem."

She stomped off to the end of the field, where she could get as
far away as possible from me.

I watched her go and felt stupid. *What the fuck is a nerve pill?*
I wondered. Then the whispering moms came up beside me.
One put her arm around me and said, "Phew, that was a little
rough, huh?"

I nodded.

The other one opened her handbag. "Need a little something
to help you feel better, sweetie?" She offered me a little blue pill.

Holy shit! I was in. I looked at the little blue pill and then into
the woman's lifeless eyes. I heard Stacy call out, "You're doing wonderful, Jaxon! I'm getting some great action shots for your scrapbook!" I realized I had no desire to scrapbook or bake or work
out—with or without pills. And no pill was going to give me a
sense of style or gorgeous carefree braids. I didn't want to take a pill
that would turn me into a cleaning zombie (although I'm sure the
Hubs wouldn't mind). I liked my mood swings, I liked my sharp
edges, and I liked feeling angry and scared and excited and angry.

I also realized that Xanax and Adderall aren't *my* mother's
little helpers. I've been downing my drug of choice for years
without ever realizing it. I'm not a pill popper. I'm a stress eater.

"No, thanks," I said. "I'll just take the rest of those muffins."

MOTHERHOOD: THE TOUGHEST COMPETITION YOU'LL EVER JUDGE

Before I had kids I'd heard grumblings about the Mommy Wars. I assumed it was working moms versus stay-at-home moms. I was sure the working moms complained that the stay-at-home moms ate bonbons and watched soaps all day, while they toiled in the office. The stay-at-home moms complained that the working moms loved their careers more than their kids. What I didn't realize then was that the Mommy Wars are so much more than working moms versus stay-at-home moms. It's just not that black and white anymore. Mommies don't compete only over who has the toughest job in the world; that would be too easy. We all "chose" our jobs and have made peace with our choice. We're tired of competing over that shit. Now we want to compete over the one job we have in common: mothering. Now the Mommy Wars are all about who can out-mom their neighbor.

The judging is no longer about who spends the most time at home with her kid or who has the most important job; it's been ratcheted up to who can breast-feed the longest and in the most unusual places (or positions—have you seen the viral picture of the naked mom standing on her head breast-feeding?), or whose child is the busiest or the smartest or sometimes the dumbest (yup, moms compete over that shit, too), or who can make the most adorable lunch that their kid will end up throwing away.

The battlefield for these Mommy Wars is the only common ground where all of these women come together for a brief afternoon: the elementary school carnival. It's the only place where the moms will be forced to "politely" interact with one another. So they put on their phoniest smiles, reach deep into their arsenal of passive-aggressive put-downs, and take their child to the school to make some damn memories.

I had the pleasure of working at the carnival once, and it was nuts. These women didn't use guns or knives to fight their war. They didn't need to—their words were deadly enough.

I started the day at the check-in booth. My job was to make sure that everyone who came through the door had paid to attend. The day before, the carnival committee had sent home wristbands in the kids' backpacks. The kids were supposed to wear the wristbands as proof of payment. I noticed a family come in and none of the kids were wearing wristbands. I approached them and said, "Hi, welcome to the school carnival. Do you have your wristbands?"

"No," the mother replied, "we never received them."

"Hmm, that's strange. They were supposed to go home in your oldest child's backpack yesterday."

"Well, we never got them."

"Okay," I said. "Let me just look at the list and see if there's a note or something." I pulled out the master list and asked for her last name.

"Cooper-Wells," she said.

I scanned the list and found the Cooper-Wells family on the

list. "Here you are. It says you've paid. I can just get you some new wristbands."

I was about to go grab some new wristbands when she stopped me. "We don't need *new* wristbands, because we *never* got them in the first place."

"Right. Like I said, I'm going to get you some new wristbands," I replied.

"You're not listening," she said. "You keep saying 'new' like *I* lost the first set. I didn't lose them. I never received them."

There was something about Mrs. Cooper-Wells that rubbed me the wrong way. She was getting on my nerves with her semantics about "new" wristbands. She was so defensive, and I wasn't even attacking her—yet. I said, "I'm not sure what happened to your wristbands, but either way, I'm happy to get you a *new* set." Yeah, I can be just as bitchy as the next person.

"You're not following," she said. "You see, I'm very organized. I have to be. I'm a working mom. I have systems in place in my house. My children have a routine. They have to, because I don't have time to dig through their backpacks and go looking for important things. I have to teach them responsibility. It's my job. I've done it well. If Harrison had received the wristbands yesterday, we'd have them today."

This is when the woman in charge of stuffing the wristbands in backpacks came over to see what the hullabaloo was about. "Everything okay over here, Jen?" she asked.

"Sort of. They don't have their wristbands."

"Are they on the list?"

"Yes."

"Okay, so let's get them some new ones."

"We don't need *new* ones," Mrs. Cooper-Wells interjected. "Because we never got them."

"Well, my committee and I stuffed the backpacks yesterday, and if your name is on the master list, then your child received the wristbands," the stuffer said.

"As I was telling her," Mrs. Cooper-Wells said, pointing at me, "I have a system in place. If my son had received the wristbands, we'd be wearing them."

Now the backpack stuffer was getting pissed. "If you're on the master list, then you received your wristbands."

"I saw your master list. There wasn't any indication of who received their wristbands, only that payment was received. I would think something as simple as a check in the margin would be helpful in letting you know that you've put those wristbands in the backpack. How do you know the wristbands went in the backpack?"

"Because *I* have a system," the stuffer growled.

Whoa. It was getting tense now. I thought Mrs. Cooper-Wells needed to back down and stop being so uptight about the wristband thing, but I also thought the backpack-stuffing lady was going to quickly cross a line and tell Mrs. Cooper-Wells to fuck off. So I decided to do what I do best: crack an ill-timed joke that's intended to make fun of myself but really makes the situation worse. "Wow, you guys are both so organized. I wish *I* had a system. My kids just dump their crap on my kitchen floor once a week and I sift through it and hope there was nothing too timely in there. We lose all kinds of stuff. If I hadn't put my wristbands on my kids yesterday as soon as they got home from school, we wouldn't have ours, either."

Mrs. Cooper-Wells glared at me and said, "Children thrive with routine and structure and systems. I can't imagine *sifting* through my kids' *stuff* once a week."

Now I was pissed. Who did this bitch think she was?

Forget the backpack stuffer crossing the line; *I* was going to cross it. "You know what?" I said. "Today my job is to check wristbands, and your family doesn't have any. I'm sorry your system didn't work and your kid lost the wristbands—don't even say he didn't, because we *all* know that's what happened. Not one other person has come in today and accused us of incompetence. The people in charge of this carnival have worked hard, and if you think you could do a better job, then by all means, please volunteer to be in charge next year. I bet no one will be missing wristbands if you and your systems are in charge. Now, here are your *new* wristbands. Enjoy your day." I handed her some wristbands and sent her and her gaping mouth on their way.

At that point the carnival chairwoman must have realized I could use a break, and she thought she was doing me a favor when she sent me to the cafeteria to help with the food line.

I found a spot at the end of the line where I could serve up tepid corn dogs and bags of popcorn.

I was immediately lectured by Kay, the first mom to arrive at my station. "I can't believe that this is what you guys are serving," she complained.

"Excuse me?" I asked. I always say "excuse me" even though I heard perfectly well what the person said. I feel that by saying "excuse me," I'm giving them a chance to realize they're being an asshole, and they can change their attitude for the second attempt.

Kay didn't get the memo. Instead she said louder and slower, "I can't believe . . . this is what you guys . . . are serving."

"Well, you don't have to eat it," I replied.

"What are our choices, though? My kids are starving and they need food. This barely qualifies. This is just processed garbage on a stick."

I couldn't argue with that statement, but did she see me eating it? No way. However, no one who comes to a school carnival expects to eat kale. What else would you eat at a carnival if not crap on a stick?

I looked around the lunchroom and saw one mom unpacking a lunch box that she'd brought from home. "Ellen brought lunch for her kids," I said. "I guess you could do that next year."

"Or next year you could serve something remotely healthy."

Really? Another helpful comment about how to run the carnival better? Did I look like a fucking suggestion box? First it was Mrs. Cooper-Wells suggesting her systems for wristbands, and now Kay with her helpful menu-planning ideas. I sighed heavily. After years of serving on the PTO, I've learned the most efficient passive-aggressive way to say "fuck you," and I use it a lot. "You know what? That is so helpful, Kay. We're always looking for volunteers at the carnival. Maybe you'd like to be in charge of the food next year? Should I go ahead and put you down?" I asked.

"I know what you're thinking. You're thinking that because I'm a stay-at-home mom I must have all the time in the world to volunteer at school," she said.

"Nope, I wasn't thinking that at all." Mostly because I was thinking what a giant pain in the ass she was and how I was so glad she never volunteered at school.

She ignored me. "Well, I don't. I have a lot I do every day. I'm very busy. If done properly, running a household is as much work as a full-time job."

"Oh yeah? Do you have systems?" I asked, egging her on. I couldn't resist. I was bored, and I enjoy a good bear-baiting.

"Systems? No, I don't have systems. I don't need systems. I just treat my roles of wife, mother, and homemaker as a job. I set goals for myself and I attain them. I hold myself accountable."

"Would you ever fire yourself if you didn't meet your goals?" Poke, poke, poke.

"I know you're making fun of me, but my job is important."

"Oh, I believe you," I said. "I suck at all of my jobs—especially the wife-mother-homemaker one. Mostly because I don't get paid for it. I tend to put my paying jobs ahead of laundry. Actually, I put my non-paying jobs ahead of laundry, too. *Anything* to avoid laundry," I said. Yup, I was trying to be funny again. Nope, it didn't work.

"Well, that's a shame, because your job as a wife, mother, and homemaker is the most rewarding job you have. Especially being a mother. You're molding little humans. You're raising our future leaders."

I shrugged and said, "Yeah, well, my future leaders won't be able to do laundry."

She shook her head sadly. "I know you don't treat motherhood with respect. Avalynn has told me about Gomer's lunches. All deli meats and pudding cups. You're slowly killing your kids, you know."

I tried to think up a witty retort about all of those preservatives in Gomer's lunch extending his "shelf life," but before I could say anything she flipped her hair and was gone—with three corn dogs and a bag of popcorn. *I hope she chokes on that shit,* I thought.

"Don't listen to her," whispered the woman next to me, serving up soda. "Hi. I'm Starr. I've known Kay since we were in La Leche League together. My daughter, Gaia, is the same age as Avalynn. For all her talk about being mother of the year, Kay only stuck with breast-feeding for three weeks. She thought it was too hard and it interfered with her workout schedule. Did you know that she works out for two and a half hours every day?

Who has time for that? And what's more important, really—worrying about fitting in your jeans right away or giving your baby the best possible start in life?"

I was too embarrassed to tell Starr I only lasted two weeks in La Leche. Those chicks were hard-core! I had a preemie with a head the size of a racquetball and my boob was closer to a watermelon. Seriously, one boob weighed more than his whole body. I couldn't stop worrying that I was going to crush him. I quit after two weeks and got my money's worth out of my breast pump.

"Well, it sounds like she's trying now. She and her kids eat really clean," I said. "Avalynn's never even had a pudding cup."

"Ha! Just because you buy organic stuff at Costco doesn't mean that you're eating clean. I have a vegetable and herb garden in my backyard. It's invaluable. Both for the health benefits and to teach my Gaia and Cedar, my son, how to nurture and love the land. Do you garden at all, Jen?"

"No. I don't think our homeowners' association allows gardens," I said, knowing full well that even if it was allowed, I'd never have a garden. I may not take much pride in my landscaping, but it still looks a shit ton better than some ugly vegetable garden.

"Excuse me," a woman interrupted me and Starr. "Do you only have corn dogs?"

Seriously? Was I going to have another discussion about how bad this shit was for her kid? "Yes," I replied. "I know it's not the healthiest choice, but it's a carnival."

"Oh, I don't care about that," she said. "I was asking because Rocket doesn't like corn dogs. He likes pizza."

I looked at the kid standing next to her. "Oh. Yeah. Sorry. No pizza. Just corn dogs and popcorn."

"I want pizza," Rocket whined at his mother.

"I know, sweetie, but the lady didn't get any pizza," she said.

"But corn dogs are gross. I want pizza!"

"Rocket, I hear you," his mother said, "and I understand your frustration. Unfortunately the people in charge decided to go with corn dogs instead of pizza."

"Pizza!"

"Honey, please don't get upset. Mama hates it when you get upset," she soothed Rocket. I wanted to smack the kid, but I could tell she was the type to press charges. "Ooh . . . I know! Why don't we find Daddy and see if he'll run out and get us a pizza?" She turned to me. "Can we do that? Can we bring in outside food?"

"Um, yes, I guess so. Ellen brought sandwiches from home, but I think she did that because her daughter has severe food allergies. We're selling corn dogs and popcorn to make money for the school. 'Cause, y'know, it's a fund-raiser."

"Right. I hear you, and I can understand how hard it is to raise money, but the thing you need to understand is that Rocket hates corn dogs and he wants pizza. Your job is to raise money, but my job is to make sure that Rocket is happy."

Out of the corner of my eye I saw Starr nodding along in agreement with this woman. I looked around, hoping that someone would transfer me to the dunk tank before I started throwing corn dogs at people. "*That's* your job? *His* happiness? Do you have other kids, too, or just Rocket?"

"I have two kids, actually," she replied. "We also have Serena."

"So what happens when it's impossible to make both Serena *and* Rocket happy?" I asked. I really was curious to know how she handled it. When your entire job is making sure your kids are happy, it can be a real shitty day at the office when your tiny "bosses" can't get on the same page. I can't imagine trying to make both Gomer and Adolpha happy at the same time about anything. If I said, "We're going out for dinner and you two can pick where we go!" one would say McDonald's and the other would say Subway. I thought maybe this woman knew something the rest of us didn't. Maybe she knew how to get *both* of her kids to answer that question with "Mexican!"

"What do you mean? I don't understand," she said, genuinely confused.

"Well, for instance, Rocket wants pizza right now, but what about Serena? What if she wants a burger? Will your husband go get pizza and a burger?"

"Yes, that's exactly what we'd do."

I restrained myself from reaching across the table, smacking her upside the head, and yelling, *What is wrong with you, woman?* Instead I said, "So, do you cook more than one meal every night?"

"Not *every* night," she said, starting to get huffy. "They'll both eat mac and cheese."

I heard Starr suck in her breath. I was sure the idea of boxed macaroni and cheese was sending her over the edge.

"It's organic!" she cried when she noticed Starr's disapproval. "It's from Costco!"

"You want to take this one, Starr?" I asked, stepping away from the table.

I needed some space. I ducked into the library to see if they needed any help supervising the raffle for the class baskets. Each grade was responsible for putting together a basket. Participants bought tickets and dropped them into the buckets beside each basket; the winners would be chosen at the end of the day.

I sat down and was checking my email when I was interrupted. "I can't believe there is a live animal in the auction," a woman named Veronica huffed at me.

"Huh? What?"

"There is a rabbit up for auction."

I looked around and saw a rabbit in a wire cage. "Oh. Yeah. There he is," I said, going back to my phone.

"What if whoever wins him has no intention of caring for him?"

"I don't know."

"Well, don't you think you should know? Aren't you on the PTO? You can't allow a live animal to go home with a family who is not capable of caring for it," Veronica said.

"I'm certain that whoever wins him will be very good to him," I assured her.

"Well, I won't be happy if I win it," a woman named Julia said, joining our conversation. "It shouldn't be in the auction."

"Look, I wouldn't be happy if I won it, either," I said. "That's why I didn't put a raffle ticket in the bucket for the bunny. If you don't want it, put your ticket in the bucket by the iPad. It's much easier to care for."

"Well, I have no idea where my children put their tickets," Julia complained. "They really wanted that rabbit, so they probably put all their tickets in that bucket."

"See? This is exactly what I was worried about. Well, at least Julia knows she can't handle a rabbit," Veronica said, "but what about everyone else? Last year the Molloys won the guinea pig and it was dead within a month."

"That's why the committee went with a bunny this year. Supposedly they're hardier," I said.

"Are you trying to be funny?" Veronica asked me.

"Sort of. Look, I agree that a rabbit is a stupid idea for an auction basket. However, the dumb thing was free, and the committee doesn't turn away free stuff—ever. If they can raffle it off for a dollar, they'll do that. I know that if someone really wanted a rabbit, it would be ideal if they thought through all of the pros and cons of pet ownership and then went to the store and bought one. But while that rabbit will probably be won by someone who has no idea what to do with it, I'm sure they'll figure it out."

"I just hope it turns out better than the Molloys and the guinea pig."

"I need to find my kids and ask them if they put their tickets in the bunny bucket," said Julia.

"Why did you let your kids put the tickets in that bucket, Julia?" I asked. "My kids wanted the rabbit, too, but I told them to put their tickets in any other bucket but the rabbit's."

"I didn't let them. They chose to," said Julia. "They are independent people who are capable of having thoughts and desires. Does anyone control you?"

"Yes. Society. We have rules and laws we have to follow."

"I mean, does anyone in your house control you?"

"No, but I'm the adult in my house. So I get to be in charge."

"Being an adult doesn't give you the right to control children. They're just smaller people, that's all," said Julia.

"Smaller people who live in my house and eat my food and expect me to buy them raffle tickets," I reminded her. "Thus I get to choose where the raffle tickets go, and I said no bunny."

"Do your children fear you?" asked Julia.

"I sure hope so," I replied. "Or else I'm doing something wrong."

"That's not funny, Jen."

For once I wasn't trying to be funny.

I sighed and put down my phone. All day long I'd listened to everyone else throw their mom-bombs at one another. It was my turn to join the war now and impart my words of wisdom that no one cared to hear. "See, what you don't understand, Julia, is that I have no problem with my kids fearing me a little bit. I'm not their friend. I'm their mother. I'm always late turning in permission slips and money for field trips, but their homework is never late. I might be killing them slowly with sugar and nitrates, but when we're in the car, they buckle up. I let my kids make decisions for themselves, but some things are not up for discussion. When it's cold, they wear a coat. Every morning and every night, they brush their teeth. And finally, they cannot have a rabbit, because I don't want to be the one stuck taking care of it. So I told them to put their tickets elsewhere, which I am confident that they did. I know I'm not alone on that last one. I think that *most* parents who purchased the raffle tickets are telling their children what they may and may not bid on. I'm sorry that your children have no rules. Maybe you should adopt some systems."

If I had long enough hair to flip, I would have done it as I turned and left the library. As soon as I hit the hall I started searching frantically for my kids. "Gomer! Adolpha!" I yelled when I spotted them. "Where did you put your raffle tickets?" The winners were going to be announced soon, and even though I'd told my kids not to put their tickets in the bunny bucket, that didn't mean they'd actually listened to me. I wasn't sure what would be worse, the shame of facing Julia after winning the damn thing or having to tell Veronica it died quicker than the Molloys' guinea pig.

WATCH IT, THAT ROOM
MOM'LL CUT YOU

Being a room mom is one of the worst jobs at elementary school, and that's coming from the lady who is currently serving as the PTO president—a job that mostly involves listening to people yell at you about things you have no control over. If you've ever been a room mom, then you know it's a job that is taken *very* seriously. It's not a job for the weak. Tough decisions must be made when you're the room mom, decisions like selecting the perfect gift for the teacher's birthday or choosing the theme for the classroom basket that will be auctioned off to the highest bidder at the school carnival.

At least it's easier to hear someone bitch, "I hate the colors of the hallways in the school. The PTO should paint them," when you're the PTO president and you have perks like your own parking spot and . . . hmm, I guess that's about it as far as perks go. Still, what do the room moms get? Nothing. Except a tiny bit of power that they can wield over their fiefdom.

Not everyone is cut out to cross a room mom, and I learned that lesson early on.

It was back-to-school night, and I was visiting Adolpha's kindergarten classroom for the first time. Her teacher had just finished telling us about all of the exciting plans she had for the year. "Well, it's been lovely meeting all of you tonight," she said. "I hope those of you who are interested in volunteering in the classroom signed up on the sheet I put out earlier."

I decided to check it out and see if she needed paper plates for anything.

The sheet was almost completely blank except for the line for room mom. Four women had written down their names. Yeah. Four. One, two, three, four. There are only three parties to plan, there are only two occasions to buy teacher gifts, there is only one carnival basket to design, yet four women wanted the job—so bad that the last two had scrawled their names in the margins of the paper. The other lines on the sign-up sheet were blank. No one was doing a craft or a game or a healthy (or unhealthy) snack for any of the parties. We just had a lot of ladies in charge of no one. I imagined that so many room moms could only be trouble. In my experience, when you get four women together all trying to make an event special for their child and his or her teacher, it can get . . . testy. Or maybe it's only testy if I'm in the group. I've been told I can be a bit pushy.

All of those names crammed onto one line sort of irked me. What were they trying to prove? I loved my kid, too, damn it. I just didn't want to prove it by elbowing my way in as room mom. I could do something, too, to make her parties special. But when I picked up the pencil I was suddenly accosted. "Hi, Jen. What are you thinking about signing up for?" asked Lucy, one of the four room moms.

"I was going to do paper plates, but I didn't see a line for that. Do you guys not need plates for anything this year?"

"I'm not sure. Plates are something we can always get at the last minute," Lucy said.

"Right. If you say so. *I* think plates are pretty important," I said. "But since you don't have plates as an option, I guess I'll do the Halloween party craft."

"Are you sure you want to do that?" she asked.

"Yeah. Why wouldn't I?"

"Well, I just didn't know you were crafty."

"I'm fairly crafty. You should see my basement. Crafting is my dirty little secret." I winked. She stared at me as if I had said my dirty little secret was running a dog-fighting ring.

I changed gears quickly. "Look, it's a bunch of little kids. How crafty do you need to be? We'll probably just make those lollipop ghost things."

"Ooh, yeah, we can't do those," she said with fake sadness.

Now she was joined by Cadence, one of her fellow room moms. "Yeah, we're doing a sugar-free party this year," Cadence said.

"A sugar-free Halloween party?" Blasphemous!

"Yes."

"You do know Halloween is all about sugar? The whole idea of Halloween is to go and collect candy from strangers."

"Jen, we have a childhood obesity problem in our country, and we don't want to add to that. We know that the kids are going to get so much junk, and we don't want to be a part of it."

"What about treats? Will there be cupcakes or anything?" I asked, because now I wanted to sign up to bring those huge Costco cupcakes.

"Oh no," Lucy said. "We're only doing healthy treats. Estelle's mom is going to make the most adorable veggie skeleton you've ever seen. The kids are just going to freak out when they see it."

"'Freak' is probably the right word," I replied. "I think most kids would freak out at a veggie-only Halloween party."

"Most parents appreciate this ban on sugar. They're *thrilled* we're doing this."

"So all four of you decided that just now?" I asked.

"No. I decided," Lucy said. "I signed up as room mom first, so I'm the head room mom. I'm the one who has to make those tough calls." Cadence looked a little shocked at Lucy's obvious power grab, but she reined it in. Got to put on a united front, I guess.

"Oh. Gotcha. Well, if I can't do lollipop ghosts, I'll figure out something else."

"Perfect!" Lucy said. "Do me a favor, though. Once you've got it planned, just shoot me an email and let me know so I can approve it."

"You want to approve my craft?"

"Well, obviously, I'm going to need to. Especially since your first idea wasn't on the approved list."

"I'll do toilet paper mummies. I just saw those on Pinterest last week. They look easy enough."

"Hmm . . . will they be scary?" asked Cadence.

"I doubt it. They have googly eyes and smiley faces." No sugar *and* nothing scary? These women were ruining my favorite holiday.

"I think that will work," said Lucy. "Just send me a link to the pin so I can check it out."

"I can show it to you on my phone right now," I replied, reaching for my phone.

"Oh, now's not a good time for me. I'm here tonight to get to know Emalyn's teacher, not to be 'room mom,'" she said, using air quotes. "I have to set work-life boundaries. In fact, go ahead and send the link to Elaine. I think I'll have all replies to my room mom correspondence go to Elaine."

Elaine was on the other side of the room, but her ears perked up when she heard her name. "Huh? You need me to do something, Lucy?" she asked.

"Yes. When I send out emails to the parents, I'm going to have all questions and replies go to you. Then you can sort through them and organize them for me. It will keep my inbox clutter down and free me up to focus on the most important job I have."

"Carnival basket?" I asked. (Hey, I was born a PTO president. My motto is "Always be fund-raising.")

"No," Lucy said disdainfully. "Teacher Christmas gift."

"So what are you thinking?" Elaine asked Lucy.

"I have an idea," offered Cadence.

"Hey, you guys," said the fourth room mom, Virginia. "I've got that questionnaire from Mrs. Johnson she's filled out with her likes and dislikes. She likes Chipotle and Target and baseball. So I was thinking maybe we could get her some gift cards and find some cool baseball memorabilia online or tickets to a game or something like that."

"No," Lucy said, dismissing her. "I've been thinking about this all summer. What does every woman love?"

"Wine," I said.

"Pampering, Jen," Lucy scolded me. "A spa day."

"Ooh, that does sound nice," I said. "I love massages and pedicures."

"Yes, except what if she could be pampered in her own classroom by her own students?"

Huh? I didn't get it.

"Who wants to take a day and go to a spa when we can bring the spa to her? I want to set up Mrs. Johnson's Spa in her classroom during lunch one day. We'll have the kids give her scalp massages and rub her feet with essential oils. We'll bring in lunch for her and give her a gift card to Barnes and Noble. Teachers never have enough books."

"Actually, they do. My cousin is a teacher and she told me that teachers get books really cheap from Scholastic," I said. "Besides, Barnes and Noble isn't on the questionnaire. Mrs. Johnson likes Target."

"Jen, why are you even a part of this conversation? You're not a room mom," Lucy said.

"Well, you guys started talking in front of me, and when you're ready to buy the gift, I'm going to be one of the people you ask to give money, so I thought I'd offer you my opinion."

"Well, this is really a conversation for room moms," Cadence said. Virginia and Elaine nodded vigorously.

I wanted to say to Virginia, *What are you looking at? You're the lowest one on this totem pole, and you'll be lucky if Lucy lets you do the game at the Winter Party. Better start brushing up on Snowman, Snowman, Reindeer!*

Now I was starting to get pissed. First I needed to get my fucking craft approved, then I was ordered to direct all of my correspondence to Lucy's lackey, and now these bitches expected my kid to run her hands over Mrs. Johnson's dry scalp? (No offense, Mrs. Johnson—my scalp is very dry, too.) I couldn't take it anymore. I said, "You know what? Your ideas are revolting, Lucy. I don't know who it's worse for—the kids who have to eat their lunch after massaging their teacher's cracked heels or the teacher who has to endure twenty sets of dirty little mitts pawing her feet while she tries to choke down her lunch, which probably isn't even Chipotle."

"Well, it's not your decision to make," Lucy sneered. "You're not a room mom. Why don't you go and start collecting toilet paper rolls for your craft? But be sure to send the link to Elaine for approval first."

"Got it," I replied.

I walked down the hall and signed up to run for PTO president. I won an uncontested race. Nobody wants to be PTO president. They'd rather fight over the room mom spots. It makes no sense. What these bitches didn't get is this: why waste your time ruling a fiefdom when you can have a kingdom—and a parking space?

WOULD YOU TAKE LESS THAN A QUARTER FOR THIS SWAROVSKI VASE?

I love garage-sale-ing. (Yes, I just used it as a verb. If you are a fellow garage sale aficionado, then you understand why and you also use it as a verb.) There is nothing that makes me happier than driving around town every fall and spring and seeing the neighborhood banners advertising upcoming garage sales. It's amazing what people get rid of. You never know what you're going to find in someone's dusty garage. I've heard folklore about long-lost engagement rings hidden in the lining of a handbag or priceless copies of the Declaration of Independence pasted to the backs of old paintings, but I've only found excellent deals on kids' soccer cleats. Still totally exciting, though. New cleats are expensive!

Besides shopping at garage sales, I love hosting garage sales. Every year my mom and I dig through our houses and find a bunch of crap (I mean really terrific stuff) to sell so we can earn some money so we can go back out and buy some more crap (I mean really terrific stuff) that we'll use for a bit and then turn around and garage-sale in a couple of years. It's the circle of life suburban style.

My mom and I take our garage-sale-ing very seriously. We set up tables and clothing racks and organize our loot like our own little store. We line the driveway with the "good" stuff meant to entice people and draw them in so they will stay awhile. We work hard to get good, quality buyers into our garage of goodies.

There are lots and lots of nice, normal people who come to our garage sale. They look around and they compliment us on our neatness (little do they know it's the only time of year I sweep out my garage), the quality of our merchandise (a lot of my mom's clothes still have the tags on them, and I sell so many designer kids' clothes that I've been known to tell people I have four children instead of two), and the overall ambiance of our garage sale (we pipe in soft music on the laptop and sell cold beverages; if you squint your eyes and ignore the lawn mower and the overflowing recycling bin, you'd *almost* think you're at the mall). The nice, normal people always pay the asking price and never say stupid things like "I'll give you twenty-five bucks to take that deep freezer off your hands," pointing to my garage freezer (plugged in and full of my family's frozen food) that is clearly marked with a sign stating that it's not for sale.

Fortunately, the nice, normal people are the ones who visit often, but sometimes my mom and I host a garage sale that attracts the jackholes of the world.

Our last garage sale started off perfectly fine, and then the mother with the tiny tornado swooped in. Look, I'm not stupid. I know my number one garage sale customer is my fellow mom. Kid gear, toys, and clothes are expensive, and my garage sales are a great place to pick up some terrific deals, so I'm always happy to see a mom and her kid walk up my driveway. *However.* This bitch was so preoccupied with pawing through my mom's pile of three-dollar jeans, she barely noticed that her demon spawn was running amok. Whenever I am irritated by a kid's behavior I always try to do the passive-aggressive thing to get the mom's attention. I'm not proud of it, but people are crazy when it comes to their kids. You can't just open with "Lady, restrain your brat, would ya?" You've got to finesse it. So I said, "I know I'm only asking a couple of bucks for that set of Legos your son is strewing across my driveway, but now that he's lost half of the pieces, I'm worried I won't even get a quarter for it."

"What?" She looked up from the pile of my mother's size 10 jeans that were never going to fit her size 14 ass (trust me, lady, I've already tried).

"Your son. He's dumping all of my Legos on the driveway."

"Aren't they for sale?"

"Yes, they are. Would you like to buy them?"

"No. We have tons of Legos."

"Well then . . ." I trailed off at this point, expecting her to do the right thing and rein her kid in, pick up the Legos, and preferably leave, because at that point she was only looking at my mom's stuff and I wasn't going to make any money off her.

"Okay," she sighed, and put down the pair of jeans she was eyeing so she could yell to her kid. "Casper! Put away the Legos."

Casper whined, "I'm just playing with them!"

"I know, baby, but the lady doesn't want you to touch her stuff. Apparently you can look but you can't touch at this sale."

Oh no she didn't! Did she just try to out-passive-aggressive *me*?

"I never said you can't *touch* the Legos. I would just prefer it if you didn't rip into the sealed box and lose half of them in my yard," I told Casper. "I'd like to sell them, and no one will want them if most of the pieces are missing."

"I want to play with them, Mommy!"

"I know, baby, but the lady says no."

You're absolutely right! The lady says no. But do you know who else should be saying no, Casper? Your damn mother.

It was around that time that Casper said, "Mommy, I have to go pee-pee!"

The negligent mother looked up at that one. "Oh! Okay, baby." Then she turned to me. "Where's your bathroom?"

Where's my what? Oh hell no. Are you fucking kidding me, lady? I don't care if your kid wets his pants. You should have handled that shit before you left the house this morning. This is a garage sale. Do I look like I've got a public bathroom? Plus, you're kind of a bitch.

I smiled at her sweetly and replied, "It's at the McDonald's right down the street."

Before she could say anything, I was interrupted. "Excuse me, do you have change for a fifty?" It was a well-dressed mother with a toddler on her hip and her Dolce and Gabbana sunglasses casually yet perfectly pushed up on her head to hold back her magnificent mane of highlighted hair. "I'm in a bit of a hurry," she continued, motioning to the idling Lexus at the curb. "I've got my baby sleeping in the car. I just wanted these things, but I don't have anything smaller than a fifty."

I looked at the items she had selected, all good Gymboree outfits with matching tights and headbands. She had about seventeen dollars' worth of stuff.

I wanted to say, *I'm on to you wily fifty-dollar people and your racket.* There are two types of fifty-dollar people. One is the Dolce mom who really looks like all she carries around are fifty-dollar bills. The other is the little old lady who says, "I just got paid and haven't had a chance to get to the bank for anything smaller." They both come early in the morning and hope to get stuff for a song because you haven't had enough sales yet to make change for them. What's really annoying is that the fifty-dollar people always grab some of my best shit. They say real sweetly, "Can you break a fifty?" while continuing to dig in their wallets as if they just might have seventeen dollars in quarters in there. And then it's like they have a great idea. "Or . . . wait . . . Hold on. Look at that." They hold up a wad of crumpled ones that look like they've either been through the washing machine or spent some time stuffed in a hooker's ass crack. "I've got three dollars. If you don't have change, that's fine. I can give you the three for all of this stuff. At least you're getting rid of it, right?"

Oh, I don't think so, wily fifty-dollar people. You can shove that dirty three dollars back up some hooker's ass, because I'm not taking that today! You can't beat me that easily. I know your tricks! And I have tricks of my own! I just went to the bank last night and got two hundred dollars in *one-dollar bills*. I can break your fifty, no problem.

I said, "You know what? I *can* break your fifty. Let's get that taken care of for you right away so you can get back to your baby. Would you like a bag for all of that? I think I even have a Gymboree one." I winked at her.

Her scheme has probably worked so many times that she's been using the same fifty-dollar bill over and over again . . . until she met me. Nothing felt better than taking her fifty out of circulation. However, one of these days I'm going to be on the losing end, because it's only a matter of time before someone slips me a counterfeit fifty.

After she left, I noticed we had some new shoppers. Great! Then I took a closer look and noticed the woman in the fifteen-year-old Christmas sweater (in April) and the man with saggy trousers held up by the poorest excuse for a belt I'd ever seen. It was an enormous belt with new holes punched in it so that the tail wound around his back. Clearly everything these two were wearing had been purchased at garage sales for a quarter or less. Tightwads! The wily fifty-dollar people are bad enough, but the worst people to come to my garage sale are the tightwads, the ones who try to talk you down lower than a quarter. Not only are they cheapskates, but they're simply assholes who want to waste everyone's time. Come on. What the fuck is worth *less* than a quarter? Nothing! If it was worth less than a quarter, then it would be in the trash, not at my garage sale. If it was worth less than a quarter, then I spent more on the sticker to mark the price. Also, I won't take less than a quarter, because I refuse to have nickels and dimes in my change box (I don't have any room with all my one-dollar bills taking up so much space).

Sure enough, the man asked, "Will you take less than a quarter for this?" He held up a crystal vase that was a wedding present. It had quite a bit of sentimental value to me. Okay, I'm lying. I think one of my co-workers gave it to us. I knew the crystal vase in the tightwad's hand wasn't Swarovski, but it was at least Macy's brand of crystal. Sure, the person who had (kindly) bought it for us probably used a coupon, and yes, it hadn't been in style for thirty years, but it was worth a quarter, damn it!

It took all of my self-restraint to say "No, sorry" instead of "No, but I hear your mom will."

Let me just stop right here and be clear that there is a difference between the tightwads and the hagglers. I'm not talking about the hagglers. I don't mind the hagglers. I get it. It's a garage sale. That's half the fun. It's a rush to walk out of someone's garage with your new treasure (their old junk) and the knowledge that you spent less than a cup of coffee to get all that swag. The only way you're going to do that is if you haggle. But you've got to play the game and play it cool. You need to look like you barely even *like* those curtains in your hand. You have to say things like, "I'm not even sure they will work in my house. I think there might be three windows in that room—I can't remember—and there are only two curtains here. I can try them, though, and just see. You wanted six dollars? Would you take three?" See what I did there? I made your curtains seem inconsequential. You don't know that I've been searching for three months for these exact curtains and I would probably pay ten dollars if you asked. Also, I didn't get all crazy with the haggle. I didn't go straight for the dick move of one dollar. I kindly split your asking price in half. Fifty percent is a good inoffensive number. The only time a haggler riles me up is when they imply my beautiful art or knickknacks are "perfect for the lake house." Sure, I'm getting rid of it, but that shit sat on my living room mantel, and now you're going to put it next to a moose head or a stuffed fish? My price is *always* firm if I hear it's going to the lake house.

The tightwad harrumphed and stormed out—without his crystal vase.

I was still irritated by the old man when a lady asked, "Do you have a dressing room?"

I know I set up a nice shop, but even the dumbest person out there would never confuse my garage with Nordstrom. I wasn't clear enough earlier when the negligent mother asked me if I had a public restroom for her kid to violate, and now this woman wanted a dressing room? What the hell, people? I was selling eighty-dollar pants for eight bucks. I could understand my shopper's hesitancy to buy pants at 90 percent off retail, and I could understand her desire to know for certain the pants would fit. However, the buyer was going to have to take a bit of a risk here.

She was going to have to use some common sense in this situation. First, she should pick them up and look at the brand. Was it a brand she wears on a regular basis? If it wasn't, then I could understand her concern. And if eight dollars for gorgeous wool flannel trousers (that I got too fucking fat to wear) was too rich for her blood, then maybe she should just keep moving. If it was a brand she wore on a regular basis, then yes, she could buy with confidence. She could know that these were the pants she normally paid eighty dollars for and that on this day she could get them for eight.

Only this lady didn't have pants. She had an armful of bras. When I was cleaning out my closet for the sale, I had a bin of bras that I'd set out that I was going to take to a women's shelter, and then I got too lazy and it was time to start my sale, so I shoved the bin under a table. I didn't realize that anyone would have the nerve to dig under my tables, but apparently the garage sale world is the Wild West and nothing is off-limits.

"No. I don't have a dressing room," I said to her. "Because . . . we're in a garage."

"How much are these?" she asked. I was dumbfounded. Do people buy used bras?

You know what? I never miss an opportunity for a sale. "One dollar each!" I said.

I heard my mother gasp. She knew it wasn't cheap to harness my tatas. I was giving those suckers away. "I was going to donate them anyway. It will save me a trip to the shelter if she'll buy them," I whispered to her. Yeah, I'm a real philanthropist.

"Hmmm . . ." The bra lady hesitated. "A dollar each. I don't know. . . . There's nowhere I can try these on?"

"No. Not for bras that I'm selling for a *dollar*. If you want, you

could probably make a spot back there behind my kids' sleds."
Surprisingly, the bra lady decided not to buy the bras. So the
shelter got them anyway. I *am* a giver!

Around midday is when the old married couples come out.
They walk through like they have all the time in the world. They
hold hands and survey our wares like they're archaeologists
looking through Tut's treasure. They pick up everything and in-
spect it, tsk-tsk over the imaginary flaws they find, then put it
back on the table. Sometimes I offer helpfully, "That's real crystal. It was a wedding gift from my boss. Just like Swarovski, and
only a quarter." After shaking their heads at my meager assort-
ment of crap, they give a little wave and walk back to their sedan
and move on to the next sale.

Midday also brings out the nuts. There's a guy who wants to
know if we have any real gold or silver that he could melt down
into "ingots," because soon our financial system will crash and
all trading will be done in ingots. I was sorry that I didn't have
any precious metals to sell him, because I would have loved to
hear what his idea of a fair price would be for a twenty-four-
karat gold necklace. I know what mine is, and it isn't a quarter.

After the alchemist comes the real crazy one. "You got any
guns?" a guy called from the end of my driveway, not even both-
ering to come any closer in case my answer was no. I realize that
I live in Kansas, where hunting is a popular pastime, but come
on! This is the suburbs! I have never been to a garage sale where
Colt .45s are displayed in a shoe box next to another box full of
discarded tools. No one just has a shotgun casually leaning up
against the wall with a sticker that says MAKE OFFER, yet at every
garage sale I host there is always one guy (never the same guy,
mind you) who casually asks for guns. I sputtered, "You mean
for sale or to protect myself out here?"

He replied, "For sale, of course. This is a garage sale, yeah?"

Yeah, it's a garage sale all right, *not* a gun show! Is it even legal to sell guns out of my garage? Are my neighbors doing that? Actually, don't tell me. I don't want to know.

At the end of the day we noticed that we'd been robbed. We weren't surprised. Something always gets stolen. It's just the way it goes. It's strange, because I don't mind when it's an adult. The adults always steal necessities. Look, if there is someone out there who is in such a desperate situation that they can't pay me two bucks for my kids' used tennis shoes and feel like they need to steal them, then there isn't much I can say except "God bless and good luck." In fact, if the person who swiped the toddler tennies had told me their story, I would have bagged up every outfit I had in their kids' sizes and all of the children's books and given it to them for free.

The criminals that drive me batshit crazy are the kids. As we were closing up for the day we had a toddler whose mother put a Dora the Explorer backpack on her to wear around while she shopped. In the end, the mother didn't buy anything and they started to leave. I saw my backpack walking down the driveway and I was torn. Was I really going to chase down a toddler for two bucks or was I going to let it go? I almost let it go. But then when they were all the way down at the end of the driveway the mother noticed the backpack. She glanced back to see if I'd noticed or if they could just keep walking, real casual-like. We made eye contact, though, and she had to admit her kid swiped my goods. "Oops! Marguerite really likes Dora," she called.

"Looks like it," I called back.

"Do you mind?" she called, gesturing at the adorable Marguerite and her big sad eyes.

"Of course I don't mind you buying my stuff," I called. "That's what a garage sale is for. That one's two dollars."

They walked up the driveway so that I could get a better look at just how cute Marguerite looked in the backpack. "I'm sorry, Marguerite," the woman said. "But the lady won't let you have the backpack."

Of course I will. For two dollars.

They stood there watching me. Marguerite was about to cry, and the woman was giving me a look that said, *Really, lady? You're going to make my kid cry for a lousy two bucks?*

I gave her a look that said, *No.* You're *going to make her cry for two bucks.*

She wouldn't take the backpack off her kid, and they just stood there staring me down. I was starting to feel uncomfortable and I could tell my will was about to break. I was going to give that kid the damn backpack! But then I resolved to stand strong. This woman was an asshole, and I didn't have any patience left. I was tired of listening to the passive parents who paraded through my garage and apologized to their kids because I asked them to be responsible. Fuck her. If she wasn't going to teach her kid, then I would. I said, "Sorry, Marguerite, you can't have the backpack for free. It's two dollars."

"Do you have change for a fifty?"

MOMS' NIGHT OUT AT THE GUN RANGE

After my stint as co-president of the local moms' group, I took a hiatus. My kids were in school full time now and I didn't need the playgroups anymore. I was busy shuttling everyone to soccer and checking homework at night. But while I might not have needed the playgroups anymore, I still needed a good Moms' Night Out every now and again. I was on the group's email distribution list and received the calendar every month. I'd have good intentions of showing up for a mani-pedi night or a guest speaker from the Society of Lady Gardeners, but I could never get my act together.

Until the night they went to the gun range.

I knew they were some badass mothers, but I didn't know they were *that* badass! We do pride ourselves on trying new things like cooking lessons or picking *Fifty Shades of Grey* for our book club selection, but for us it was a whole new experience. One of our members is in the Army Reserve and she had the idea that we should go shoot some guns for Moms' Night Out.

When I got the email reminding me to RSVP for the event, I

thought, *Wow, that's crazy that they're going to the range.* A wine tasting is a wild night for our group, so I couldn't imagine us at the gun range. I never thought I'd go. I hate guns. I'm afraid of guns. I don't like to be around guns. Also, I have a sneaking suspicion that if I shoot a gun I will want to buy one.

"Isn't that funny that they're going to the gun range?" I asked the Hubs.

"You should *totally* go!" he said. Hold on. The Hubs never encourages me to go to Moms' Night Out.

"You want me to go because you think I'll like it and then I'll let you buy a gun," I said.

"Pretty much," he agreed.

"You know what? I'm going to go! If nothing else, maybe I'll accidentally shoot myself in the foot and have something to write about on my blog for tomorrow."

The night of the event arrived and I started to get ready to go out. As you know by now, I don't normally care how I dress— usually it's cargo pants and tees—but the range got me thinking. What does one wear to ladies' night at the gun range? Would camouflage cargos be a better choice? Maybe tweed? (I told you I watch a lot of *Downton Abbey* and they love to shoot in their tweed.) Maybe I should wear something lighter so my black gun would stand out against my ensemble. Unremarkably, I settled on the usual. Why start getting fancy now?

I met the other ladies at the gun range and we stood in the showroom giggling nervously. I had never been surrounded by so many guns in my life.

It freaked me out no end to know that everyone in the room (except for the six of us) was packing heat. I said something about this, and my friend Joni replied, "Yeah, but it's not like they've got real bullets, right?"

I laughed at her stupid question because I knew the answer. What I didn't mention was that I knew the answer to her stupid question because I had asked the Hubs the same exact stupid question just before I walked out the door.

"Wait, those are real bullets we're going to be shooting?" I'd wondered.

"*Of course,* Jen. What else would they be?" he told me.

"I don't know. I thought they were blanks or something."

"How can you hit a target with a blank? Don't be so dumb. Those are real bullets."

"Well then, what the hell keeps us from accidentally shooting one another?"

"*Nothing.* So please be careful and follow the rules."

After perusing the range's store and noticing the quality of the NRA Second Amendment RangePacks, we met our instructor, Andy. Andy had a holstered gun and a large knife on his belt just in case his gun jammed and he needed to finish the job. Plus he was a big guy who looked like he could kill you with his bare hands if all else failed. Basically, if *Red Dawn* ever happens, I want Andy on my team. "Wolverines!"

Andy took one look at our group of middle-aged minivan-driving moms and sighed deeply. "Have *any* of you fired a weapon?" he asked hopefully.

"I have," said our reservist. "But I'm not very good."

"I'm pretty good with a Nerf gun," I said.

Andy looked disgusted.

"Okay, ladies," he said with another sigh. "Let's find a conference room and give you a lesson or two before we even step out on the range."

We sat down for about twenty minutes while Andy explained the different mechanisms on the 9 mm guns we'd be using.

After passing an unloaded gun around the table for us all to try holding and working, Andy decided he couldn't postpone live ammunition any longer.

Twenty minutes didn't seem like enough time, and I was a little worried for Andy. "Do you want to put on a bulletproof vest, maybe?" I asked him.

"Nah. I'm not afraid of you guys. You'll be fine. *But* I won't be happy if someone accidentally shoots me, so be careful out there."

Andy handed out our "eyes and ears" (that's gun range talk for sunglasses and earphones) and our box of ammo and took us to the range. Lock and load, mofos!

Holy shit! If I'd been nervous in the store, surrounded by unloaded guns on display and holstered guns on people, I was terrified in the range, where guns were actually firing. Andy gave us all a reassuring smile and told us we were going to have fun.

"Yay," I said weakly.

"Who's first?" he asked.

"I'll go first, but I just want to shoot one bullet," Joni said. This is the woman who didn't know we'd be shooting real bullets.

"But you have ten rounds," Andy said.

"Yeah, but I just want to shoot one," she replied. "I'm a little afraid." You and me both, sister.

"Just try it," Andy said.

She went into her lane and loaded her magazine clip. She took her stance (knees slightly bent, leaning forward, arms slightly bent, double grip on the gun) and fired. *Boom!*

A fucking head shot.

She turned around and told us, "I think I'll take another shot." She gave us a little smile, then turned back to her target. *Boom,*

boom, boom. She unloaded all ten bullets in her target's head. She looked like John McClane in *Die Hard.* Yippee-ki-yay!

"Ha! Great grouping," Andy yelled, giving her a high-five. "Who's next?"

Throughout the night we all took turns until we went through our box of bullets.

I was the worst shot. I'd like to blame it on the fact that I'm a lefty, but I know the truth is that I couldn't get my hands to stop shaking. Every time I picked up that gun I felt nervous and queasy. When I was in the lane and someone was firing next to me I jumped every single time. I couldn't get over how deadly these weapons were and how I was just trusting everyone in that room to not shoot me.

Even though I was the worst shot, I still shot my "victim" dead. (I kept calling my target a "victim," and then Andy reminded me I should probably call it an "assailant"; otherwise that makes me a crazy person who just shoots people.)

I was stunned by how easy it was to hit the target. I'd been sure I'd be lucky if I hit the target once or twice, but I only missed my victim—er, assailant—two or three times. The rest of the time I gravely wounded him.

By the end of the night we were feeling like a mix of *Charlie's Angels* and *Full Metal Jacket.* It was a high, and we were a bit amped up by our success. We all took our targets home to show our husbands that they shouldn't mess with us!

I was surprised, but we actually had a great time hanging out together, laughing, and being badasses and just plain asses. I'm glad I tried it. None of us bought a gun that night. I still have a healthy fear of and respect for guns, and I still don't want one. I'm not convinced I could ever use it properly. If I was truly under attack, I would most likely freeze up or accidentally shoot the wrong person. I posted on my Facebook page that I was going to the range, and my brother, C.B., replied, "Ladies don't shoot. Ladies stab." I have to say I think he might be right, especially when it comes to me. I've decided that when the zombie apocalypse comes, I'll be grabbing a machete. That way I won't lose any time reloading.

Acknowledgments

Acknowledgments are kind of tough, aren't they? What if you accidentally forget someone? Like my parents. I will probably forget my parents so I'm just going to go ahead and thank them now. Thanks, Mom and Dad, for loving me and doing the best you could. Don't worry, I'm not *that* screwed up. And I'm sorry for all of the *f*-bombs, Mom. Let's just say Dad taught me how to swear.

Or worse, what if you go out of your way to mention someone and they never read this book and have no idea how much they mean to you? I'm looking at you, Tina Fey. Hey girl, we could totally be besties. Let's have a hoagie together—my treat. Call me.

Of course, I have to thank my husband. I know I already dedicated the book to him, but he's going to want a mention here, too. Plus, he totally deserves it. This book would not be possible without him. While I wrote furiously to meet every deadline, he was the one who kept our children fed and moderately clean, while at the same time he motivated me and kept me sane. Thank you, Hubs, for understanding, supporting, and loving me even though I am such a pain in the ass. You are my lobster. Oh, and thank you for buying me a badass minivan.

Thank you, Gomer and Adolpha, for letting me give you terrible names and tell funny stories about you. Someday you'll read this book and we'll laugh together and then you'll send me your therapy bills.

Thank you to Neeti Madan and Pamela Cannon for helping me with this book.

Thank you to my local McDonald's for having the most delicious Coke on the planet and free refills and '80s music on a loop, because nothing inspires me like caffeine and Bananarama.

Thank you to every member of my tribe of bloggers and writers who has ever shared my work. Together we can do amazing things! When the water rises all of the boats rise!

And last, but certainly not least, thank you, thank you, thank you to my readers. You make dreams come true. Without you none of this would be possible. Your support has been incredible and I am so lucky to have each one of you. Thank you for reading and laughing.

In addition to her blog, People I Want to Punch in the Throat, which she started in 2011, JEN MANN has also written for *The Huffington Post, Babble, Circle of Moms,* and *CNN Headline News.* She was voted Best Parenting Weblog in the 2014 Bloggie Awards and was a finalist for two Bloggies in 2013 (Weblog of the Year and Best Parenting Weblog). She was voted one of *Circle of Moms*'s Top 25 Funniest Mom Blogs for 2012 and 2013 and was chosen by the same site as one of the "Most Influential" bloggers. She was a BlogHer 2012 and 2013 Voice of the Year. In 2012 her self-published debut collection of essays, *Spending the Holidays with People I Want to Punch in the Throat,* rose to the number one spot in Amazon's Humor category. She lives in Overland Park, Kansas, and is married to "the Hubs" and is the mother of two children, whom she calls Gomer and Adolpha on her blog—she swears their real names are actually worse. Find her on Facebook and Twitter.

www.peopleiwanttopunchinthethroat.com

ABOUT THE TYPE

This book was set in Minion, a 1990 Adobe Originals typeface by Robert Slimbach. Minion is inspired by classical, old-style typefaces of the late Renaissance, a period of elegant and beautiful type designs. Created primarily for text setting, Minion combines the aesthetic and functional qualities that make text type highly readable with the versatility of digital technology.